*Stare up at such a building and it fairly dominates one's mind and body.*

Frederick Simpich

**Dedication**

For my family: my husband, Don, my two daughters, Dria and Eilis, and my son, Teague, but most of all for my mother and father.

**Acknowledgments**

Special thanks to Professor William Morgan, professor of architecture at Roger Williams University, and also to Lydia K. Ruth, director of public relations for the Empire State Building, and reference librarians at Jervis Library in Rome, New York. Special thanks also to my husband, Don, for reading chapters and making suggestions for improvements.

The author and publisher gratefully acknowledge permission to use *Purple* by Roland Maycock, *Blood* by Leonard A. Hoffman, *Shades* by Paul J. Elkin, and *I Saw You Empire State Building* by Edwin Torres.

# Thirteen Months to Go

## The Creation of the Empire State Building

### Geraldine B. Wagner

Thunder Bay
P·R·E·S·S

San Diego, California

THUNDER BAY
P · R · E · S · S

Thunder Bay Press
An imprint of the Advantage Publishers Group
5880 Oberlin Drive, San Diego, CA 92121-4794
www.thunderbaybooks.com

ISBN 1-59223-105-5
Library of Congress Cataloging-in-Publication Data available upon
request.

This book was designed and produced by
Quintet Publishing Limited
6 Blundell Street
London N7 9BH, U.K.

Color separation by Universal Graphics, Singapore
Printed in China by Leefung-Asco Printers Ltd

1 2 3 4 5 07 06 05 04 03

Senior Project Editor: Corinne Masciocchi
Editor: Madeline Perri
Designer: Roger Fawcett-Tang
Art Director: Sharanjit Dhol

Creative Director: Richard Dewing
Publisher: Oliver Salzmann

# Contents

The Statue of Liberty symbolizes the dream of New York as a safe haven.

The Empire State Building symbolizes the power and style of the town.[1]

*At the time of the Great Depression, New York
was a strange brew of contradictory energies:
a business capital for the wealthy and a sink
of iniquity for those who would never be.*

New York City, the symbol of so many things to so many people, has been nicknamed the Big Apple since the 1920s when the term, commonly used by stablehands when they referred to New York City racecourses, was popularized by horseracing columnist John J. FitzGerald. His *Morning Telegraph* column, which he named "Around the Big Apple," was a big hit with the New York City racing scene. In the 1930s, jazz musicians picked up the term and used it to identify the city as the world's jazz capital. Soon the nickname became synonymous with New York City in all its cultural diversity.[2]

Few can think of the 1930s in the Big Apple without recalling at least two cultural incongruities of that era: first, the Great Depression, a time of severe unemployment, loss of life savings when banks failed, and ruined businesses; and second, the monumental and, at the time, costly construction of "the mightiest peak of New York's mighty skyline, tallest of all tall buildings…the Empire State." [3]

The Empire State Building remains perhaps the most famous skyscraper in a city famous for them. Even when the towers of the World Trade Center eclipsed it in height, the Empire State Building remained iconic, a cherished symbol of New York held in high esteem by the city's millions of residents. Since the destruction of the World Trade Center on September 11, 2001, of course, no one can look at tall buildings in quite the same way again. They are no longer invulnerable—but perhaps their emotional value is now more evident. This may be particularly true of the Empire State Building, which was built amid unlikely circumstances during the American Depression of the early twentieth century.

How these two events—the Great Depression and the construction of the world's greatest tall structure—were able to occur simultaneously still causes wonder in the American people.

Indeed, Manhattan has always been a place, as Oscar Wilde put it, where one might dine easier than where one might dwell, and at the time of the Great Depression, New York was an especially strange brew of contradictory energies at once glamorous and corrupt, diverse and forgiving, a business capital for the wealthy and those who wished to be, and a sink of iniquity for those who never would be.

Even before the economic downturn that began in the late 1920s, it was obvious to the observer that New York was made up of the haves and the have-nots, and a few other categories in the gray areas between. "On the island of Manhattan," wrote E. Idell Zeisloft, author of *The New Metropolis* at the turn of the century, "the people may be divided into seven classes: the very rich, the rich, the prosperous, the well-to-do comfortable, the well-to-do uncomfortable, the comfortable or contented poor, and the submerged or uncomfortable poor."[4]

Apparently, the president of the United States at the time, Herbert Hoover, hadn't noticed this stratification when he stated early in 1929 that "we in America today are nearer to the final triumph over poverty than ever before in the history of any land. The poorhouse is vanishing from among us."[5]

In 1929, John Jacob Raskob, chief executive of General Motors, head of the Democratic National Committee, and soon to be the principal driver in the plan to construct the Empire State Building, wrote in the *Ladies Home Journal* that "everybody ought to be rich" by investing $15 a week in common stocks. However, as the average worker's weekly salary was only about $17 a week, Raskob's enthusiastic advice should only have reached perhaps two of the seven class layers of American society. Unfortunately, like today's lottery ticket purchasing, perhaps those least able to afford such compulsive buying were the ones most likely to do so.

However, in October 1929, a stock market crash turned everything on its head. Perhaps this unbridled enthusiasm with the stock market, propped up by new investors entering the market as an easy way to get rich quick, helped bring its demise. Although Wall Street analysts of the day had their doubts, people mindlessly singing songs like "Happy Days Are Here Again" were buying stocks "on margin," that is, on credit. Even industries were overproducing and banks were lending money left, right, and center so customers could get a new car loan or buy stocks. Unknowingly, people were seeing a mere mask of prosperity when they looked in the mirror.

This so-called psychology of consumption fed the optimism of investors and gave them an all-absorbing faith in prosperity. When the crash finally came, taking the national income from $87 billion in 1929 to a low of $40 billion in 1933, the impact was that much more devastating and perplexing.

While minorities, unskilled workers, and the aged were affected most severely by the Depression, nearly everyone was forced to make sacrifices. Young couples planning to get married and waiting for the man's weekly salary to increase shrugged when it was instead cut back—and married anyway.

Many Americans suffered a host of problems, including loss of employment but also the breakdown of families, soaring high school dropout rates, homelessness, settlements of cardboard and tar-paper shacks called "Hoovervilles," farmers marching on local banks armed with pitchforks and, sometimes, guns to prevent foreclosures, and the first protest march on Washington by World War I veterans who were not getting their pensions.

College graduates pumped gasoline, former businessmen sold pencils and apples on street corners, people stood in breadlines to get their meal for the day, and hoboes jumped on freight trains as their means of escape.

*Herbert Hoover won the 1928 presidential election, running against former NYS governor Al Smith who, casting about for a new endeavor, became one of the promoters of what would become the Empire State Building.*

*Many Americans suffered a host of problems, including loss of employment but also the breakdown of families, soaring high school dropout rates, homelessness, and settlements of cardboard and tar-paper shacks called "Hoovervilles."*

*Beside the city's opulence, cardboard and tar-paper settlements during the Depression years came to be known as Hoovervilles, where the down and outs found themselves as a last resort.*

Even children were affected in their Depression-era play. They made up games like one called Going on Relief. One player acted as a relief worker, questioning her friends about their families and hearing sad stories, probably those they heard adults telling. Another game was called Picketing, where the children carried crude signs, marched back and forth, hooted at "scabs," and otherwise mimicked labor clashes they had seen or heard about from their parents.

But while the Depression was a time of hardship for many, it was also an exciting time in both New York and throughout the rest of the world. New York was a cosmopolis, bursting with energy, verve, and intensity. It was a city in full expansion.

## The Growing Metropolis

In the 1930s, the combined length of New York's residential and business telephone lines could stretch from Earth to the moon 35 times. The city burned 21 million tons of coal a year. It had more than 1,500 churches, and its citizens spoke scores of languages. Some 5,000 watches were pawned each day, and 500,000 people were arrested each year. The rest of the world was also undergoing metamorphosis and self-reflection. The human and civil rights movement for minorities and working men and women was in full force. There were scientific advances and political upheavals in Europe. The Mafia was controlling the illegal liquor trade in New York. And bridges, the new cross-river transport, were linking this city of contradictions and promise to its neighbors.

*Cimarron*, by Edna Ferber, became a best-seller while Theodore Dreiser was publishing *Tragic America*. Literary censorship increased, and customs officials seized James Joyce's *Ulysses* on the grounds that it was obscene. Leon Trotsky's work was banned in Boston. The Jehovah's Witnesses formed from the International Bible Students Association, and Norman Angell and Harold Wright were asking, "Can governments cure unemployment?"

"Time on My Hands" became one of the popular songs of the day and a slogan or catchphrase for the unemployed.

Wealthy New York developers were helping build some of the city's most monumental and memorable structures, including Rockefeller Center and the George Washington Bridge, and fueling the phenomenon of tall buildings.

Among all this came the Empire State Building—its concept born as a contest between two industrial moguls, both leaders in the American automobile industry, who wanted the status of having constructed the tallest building in the world. Ultimately, Empire State became the center of a competition between Walter Chrysler of the Chrysler Corporation and John Jacob

*Walter Chrysler in the 1920s. The automobile, a symbol of American materialism, was demanding a new infrastructure of roadways, bridges, and tunnels.*

Raskob, who helped make General Motors a fierce competitor in the upstart automobile industry. Ironically, the crazed expenditure of capital for their little contest coincided with the onset of one of the worst U.S. economic downturns of all time.

Perhaps it was the timing as much as anything else that caused such a stupendous stir in 1930 over the Empire State. "Probably no building in the history of the world has brought about such universal interest in its progress," said President Herbert Hoover about the Empire State Building.[6]

*Wealthy New York developers not only built some of the most monumental structures on Manhattan Island, they also built bridges like the George Washington Bridge to connect the city with its neighbors.*

*In comparison with today's lofty New York skyline, commerce that relied on the ocean and rivers caused buildings to spring up close to the harbor in early New York.*

*When all was said and done, there was little place else to go on the narrow island of Manhattan but toward the sky.*

Bank of the Manhattan Co.
Wall Street
New York City

*At the beginning of the Great Depression, there was a three-way skyscraper race under way in Manhattan. The Bank of Manhattan rose to 925 feet; the Chrysler to 1,048 feet; and John J. Raskob added five stories to his Empire State and later added a 200 foot mast for a total height of 1,250 feet.*

*The Chrysler Building has often been considered the prettier sister, although lacking in stature, of its contemporary, the Empire State Building.*

## Looking Up

Prior to 1900, none of the world's major cities, including New York, featured such a thing as a skyline. It took Manhattan Island, once a part of the New World wilderness, over a century to gain the population to equal that of today's small cities. When commerce began that relied on the waterways, buildings sprang up close to the harbor, but the rest of the island remained common land and farms. Little did early Manhattanites know that the fishing hole from which they pulled sunfish and eels would someday lie beneath the entrance to the world's tallest building, at the foot of the Empire State's tower express elevators.

In 1886, an enterprising architect named Cass Gilbert talked New York City officials into stretching the building code for his newfangled Tower Building, probably the city's first skyscraper. When he got his way, his neighbors were none too happy. As the building grew taller, eventually reaching a whopping 13 stories, skeptics waited for it to topple over. The owner of a neighboring building was said to have sold his property and gotten out of the way.

Gilbert was vindicated when a storm bringing gale winds with a force of 80 miles per hour hit New York. People were sure the building would be knocked over, but Gilbert reportedly climbed up into the building and showed that not only was the structure sturdy, it wasn't even vibrating. He proved his building's safety beyond reasonable doubt, and real estate developers and their speculating friends began looking not across the street so much as up toward the clouds.

Manhattan Island comprises only 22 square miles. When New Yorkers found themselves a tad too close to their neighbors, instead of turning a corner, they headed upward and called it a skyscraper. Building up instead of out seemed a good way to cram everyone and everything into that coveted space. On the other hand, perhaps the drive to build skyscrapers had more to do with New York's rivalry with Chicago, which boasted structures such as the Manhattan Building, built in 1891; the Heyworth Building, built in 1904; and the Palmolive Building, completed in 1929. In any event, in the early 1900s, for some quirky reason perhaps only the wealthiest can fathom, the race to the skies began. Industrial moguls competed to own the tallest and the grandest building in the world.

Soon, Gilbert's Tower Building was dwarfed by structures like the Woolworth Building of 1913, which boasted 60 stories. Then came the 927-foot Bank of Manhattan Building in 1930, which was bumped quickly from first place by the Chrysler Building, whose 185-foot spike, assembled in secret, stretched it 119 feet taller than the Bank of Manhattan and even taller than the Eiffel Tower in Paris. But before anyone could enjoy the pause that refreshes, along came the Empire State Building.

New Yorkers are used to change; one might even say they thrive on it, especially in the fast-changing industrial climate of Manhattan. In 1930, nine million people were eating, sleeping, laboring, and playing atop its accommodating granite surface. New York was bursting forth.

The development of the city's now-famous skyline was fated because even in an area of the United States where earthquakes can snap the coastline from Maine to Virginia like sheets being folded from the line, even minor tremors are virtual strangers to New York City itself. The geological explanation is that the shallow glaciers formed by the Ice Age weren't heavy enough to produce the rock faults that lead to massive upheavals in surrounding areas. Manhattan is a solid island—not just a hunk of granite but a mother lode of some 170 kinds of semiprecious stones. These are uncovered from time to time in the strangest places—like the garnet crystal that someone was using for a doorstop! (It was eventually moved to the American Museum of Natural History.)

But the really important stone for the Empire State Building and its lofty neighbors is Manhattan schist, which is full of that shiny mica that makes it sturdy and hard. Without this schist, some say, no building in Manhattan could have risen above six stories. Thus, in the island's topography and geography is a nature-engraved invitation to build as high and as densely as one would like. Builders were thus unconstrained by the limited square mileage of the island.

When all was said and done, there really was little place else to go to accommodate rapid growth. At first, development moved north toward uptown and the Harlems, but inevitably it had to go skyward, straight up. Eventually, New York had so many skyscrapers that people traveled farther vertically, in elevators, mile for mile, than they did in cars, trains, taxis, buses, and subways combined.

Yes, Manhattan's rampant growth inspired real estate speculation, some of it grand, bold, a gamble. The construction of the Empire State Building became not only for its developers but also for the workers and craftsmen who walked, crawled, climbed, and swung along its steel lengths a "daring adventure," a challenge to ingenuity and strength, a "gallant reaching for the heights."

Because of the spunk and hardihood of so many people, the world gained the most wonderful view obtainable without actually flying, at the top of the Empire State Building.

So, why does the Empire State Building still appeal to so many? It is an icon of New York, to be sure. But especially today, the Empire State is a symbol of the American spirit, of a steadfast determination to achieve the impossible.

*Probably no building in the history of the world has brought about such universal interest in its progress.*
President Herbert Hoover

Before even a spade full of earth was turned for Empire State, even before a stone of the old Waldorf was dislodged in the demolition operations, Empire State was built, complete—on paper.

The architects knew exactly how many beams and of what lengths, even how many rivets and bolts would be needed. They knew how many windows Empire State would have, how many blocks of limestone, and of what shapes and sizes, how many tons of aluminum and stainless steel, tons of cement, tons of mortar. Even before it was begun, Empire State was finished entirely—on paper.[1]

# Chapter 1: A Simple Pencil Design

*When John J. Raskob met Al Smith, Smith asked for his help for the 1928 presidential campaign against Herbert Hoover (pictured). Raskob resigned from General Motors and became Chairman of the Democratic National Convention.*

*Getting ready to campaign for the 1928
presidential election, Al Smith turned the
governorship of New York to Franklin
D. Roosevelt in order to run for president.*

*1928 U.S. presidential contender Al Smith
and his National Chairman, John J. Raskob.
The two later joined forces to build and
promote the Empire State Building.*

## The Deal

Sky's-the-limit real estate schemes were anything but new in 1920s New York. Al Smith, a former governor of New York State who had lost a 1928 presidential bid against Herbert Hoover, had been casting about for several months, looking for a new job. Like the Empire State Building itself, which eventually sprouted from what had been a farm field, Smith had humble beginnings. Born in a tough Irish neighborhood of fishmongers below the Brooklyn Bridge, he was a cog in the Tammany Hall political machine and watched his friends get very, very rich in both legitimate and under-the-table schemes. Perhaps either way, Smith was eager for a share of the pie.

Smith convinced a couple of his buddies, who happened to be two of America's richest men, to invest $16 million in some land and to sink a further $44 million to complete a skyscraper that would become the tallest building in the world. Pierre S. du Pont, chairman of Delaware's E. I. du Pont de Nemours and Company (originally a gunpowder manufacturer), and financier John Raskob joined Smith in developing the Empire State Building. Rising some eighty stories above Fifth Avenue on the site of the old Waldorf-Astoria Hotel, it was one of the largest real estate undertakings in the history of the country.

Pierre du Pont may have known business like Rockefeller knew oil, but he was not an expert in real estate. John Raskob, a high school dropout who had gone to work as a stenographer at $5 per week to support his family,[2] had become a secretary to du Pont. Raskob was an astute investor who, upon earning du Pont's admiration, helped his boss make stock investments in the General Motors Corporation. This turned out to be good advice. Soon General Motors was booming. Du Pont took it over and appointed Raskob vice president and finance chief. It was Raskob who invented installment payments for automobile buyers, an idea that colors the industry to this day. And it was Raskob, of all the wealthy investors in the project, who was actively involved in planning the Empire State Building.

Al Smith asked Raskob for his help on the 1928 presidential campaign against Herbert Hoover. Smith had just turned over the governorship of New York State to Franklin D. Roosevelt in order to run for president. Raskob resigned from General Motors (and, apparently, the Republican Party) and became chairman of the Democratic National Convention.

Smith was the favorite presidential candidate of many, a likable fellow who had risen from the tenements of New York. However, being a Roman Catholic was, at that time, a liability. Hoover was a political unknown, but at least he was Protestant. In the looming shadow of Prohibition, Smith was considered "wet." The upshot was that Smith was defeated.

Raskob went in search of ventures and of a way to spend his millions. He decided, for reasons unknown, to go along with Smith's speculative real estate idea. However, the stock market crash of 1929 made speculators pause to weigh the consequences of going ahead with their plans. To back down would mean taking a sure loss; continuing would risk a still greater loss.

*The Empire State Building, in comparison to other cohort architectural work like Rockefeller Center, was largely ignored by the top architects of the day.*

Waiting any longer would mean tying up an investment of $50 million without profits for too long. What to do?

Apparently, a loan for $27.5 million from Metropolitan Life Insurance Company clinched the deal. The speculators—among them Raskob and Smith but also Louis G. Kaufman, president of Chatham and Phoenix National Bank and a member of the board of directors of General Motors; Ellis P. Earle, a New Jersey politician who was active in the Republican Party; and Pierre du Pont—decided to go for it with gusto. They formed a corporation called Empire State, Inc., and named as president Al Smith, the four-time governor of New York State, and as vice president Robert C. Brown, a General Motors executive.

The firm Shreve, Lamb, and Harmon directed the architecture and supervisory work, and the company of Starrett Brothers and Eken oversaw the construction of the skyscraper, a "monument to their vision and business genius."[3]

But the Empire State Building, in comparison to other cohort architectural work like Rockefeller Center, was largely ignored by the top architects of the day. During its construction and for long after, Rockefeller Center brought much renown to New York and caused its own stir within the architectural field, which the Empire State never did to quite the same degree. Yet Empire State captures the popular imagination and as such, endures as a symbol of the people of New York.

### When Cloud Ticklers First Scraped the Sky

The term "skyscraper" was coined in the 1880s, shortly after the first tall buildings were constructed in the United States—but the history of tall buildings dates back hundreds of years. Take, for example, what some call one of the world's most significant buildings—the Ditherington Flax Mill built in 1796 in Shrewsbury, England—where one thousand men and women mechanically spun flax, shipped by barge from Ireland, into linen and yarn to make uniforms during the Napoleonic Wars. The Ditherington Flax Mill was the first multistory iron-framed structure built anywhere; it is, therefore, considered by many the mother and father of every other skyscraper in the world.

Tall towers, with thick walls of heavy stone, predate iron-framed structures. Anyone who has visited an ancient tower in Europe or elsewhere has experienced its cold, dark, tiny rooms. If the builder put in too many windows, the tower was weakened. No doubt a handful of these early structures did tumble before designers became the wiser.

*Flatiron Building caption*

*George Fuller's company also built the landmark triangular shape Flatiron Buildir in New York in 1902.*

*Some say the 1889 Tacoma Building in Chicago by George Fuller was the first structure ever built where the outside walls did not carry the weight of the building.*

*When it opened in 1913, architect Cass Gilbert's 793-foot Woolworth Building was considered a leading example of tall building design.*

**Hearts of Steel**

During the Industrial Revolution, engineers began experimenting with a new iron material: steel. An Englishman, Sir Henry Bessemer, invented in the 1800s the first process for mass-producing steel inexpensively. An American, William Kelly, had held a patent for a method of steel production known as the pneumatic process of steel making, whereby air is blown through molten pig iron to oxidize and remove unwanted impurities. Bankruptcy forced Kelly to sell his patent to Bessemer, who had been working on a similar process for making steel. In 1885, Bessemer patented a decarbonization process that utilized a blast of air; the technology is still used in the making of modern steel, known as the prince of ferric metals.

With dependable steel came the first modern skyscrapers. The term was first used during the 1880s, shortly after buildings higher than ten stories were built in the United States. Skyscrapers utilized several functional innovations: steel structure, elevators, central heating, electrical plumbing pumps, and the telephone.

The invention of the skyscraper is sometimes credited to George A. Fuller, who worked on solving the problems of the load-bearing capacity of tall buildings. Using Bessemer steel beams, Fuller created steel cages that supported all the weight in tall buildings or skyscrapers. Scholars and historians still argue about which building was the first true skyscraper—the Home Insurance Company Building in Chicago, by William LeBarron Jenney, or the Tacoma Building in Chicago, which Fuller built in 1889. Some say the latter was the first structure ever built where the outside walls did not carry the weight of the building. The Tacoma was demolished in 1929, just before construction began on the Empire State Building. Fuller's company also built the Flatiron Building in New York in 1902. When it opened in 1913, architect Cass Gilbert's 793-foot Woolworth Building was considered a leading example of tall building design.

For a building to be a skyscraper, said William Starrett, one of the Empire State builders, it must be constructed on a skeleton frame, now almost universally of steel, but with the signal characteristic of having columns in the outside walls (the steel columns beneath the curtain-wall skin), thus rendering the exterior we see simply a continuous curtain of masonry penetrated by windows.

Flat Iron Building, New-York.

*For a building to be a skyscraper it must be constructed on a skeleton frame, now almost universally of steel, but with the signal characteristic of having columns in the outside walls (the steel columns beneath the curtain-wall skin), thus rendering the exterior we see simply a continuous curtain of masonry penetrated by windows.*

William Starrett

**These are the essential characteristics of a skyscraper:[4]**
• Desires, conscious or unconscious, that a tall form expresses
• Great height
• Interior arrangement in stories
• Utmost space and light
• Skeletal framing using steel and fireproofing
• Passenger elevators
• High value of land, availability of labor and capital
• Vigorous enterprise, organization of labor
• Availability of suitable tools, processes, and sources
 of power
• A liking (or in Manhattan's case, a need) for height,
 a preference for it to lower buildings

**And here is the chronology of technology developments that enabled the skyscraper to become a reality:[5]**
1853: Elisha G. Otis's safety elevator
1855: Bessemer process for steel
1868: typewriter
1876: mimeograph (today's equivalent of a photocopier)
1876: telephone
1879: electric light
1880: steel becomes cheap
1885: the skyscraper comes into its own

   The same kind of steel frame that gives bridges the ability to span distances without bending allows skyscrapers to resist the compression of their many tons. Steel is the material that can withstand such stress, but it is not always pretty to look at. Therefore, buildings hide their torsos with a layer of skin, much like human skin. This cladding, a façade of glass, aluminum, stone, brick, or more steel, keeps weather elements on the outside of the building, where they belong.
   The period between the construction of the first tall buildings in New York City and the beginning of the Great Depression is considered one of the greatest in American architecture, "the Golden Age of Skyscrapers," when the profession of architecture and schools of architecture were firmly established,[6] and when the skyscraper became distinctively American.

*Plan K is Empire State, five floors and five floors only, cover the whole area of the location [the base of the building]. The full set back requirements of the zoning law were applied, not as height made them incapable, but in one gorgeous gesture and at the height of only five floors from the street.*

Empire State Building Planners

*Workers on the Empire State Building can look down on the dwarfed Chrysler Building, itself considered a spectacular spectacle of a building amongst the New York City skyline.*

**Empire State Design Plan A, B, C…K!**

William F. Lamb, an architect at the firm of Shreve, Lamb, and Harmon, was chosen to design the Empire State Building, considered one of the greatest feats of construction not just during this golden age but also in the all-time history of buildings. He is said to have based most of his design on the simple pencil, the clean, soaring lines of which inspired him.

As the story goes, Raskob pulled a thick pencil out of a drawer, held it up to Lamb, and asked, "Bill, how high can you make it so that it won't fall down?"[7]

Raskob had initially planned a 30-story office building on the site, but other buildings were already going beyond that height. Developers then thought that eighty stories would make their building the tallest. But then the Chrysler Building went higher, so they lifted the Empire State to 85 stories. This made the Empire State only four feet higher than the Chrysler, but a small spire, made in secret and popped on top, would increase those measly four feet in an instant.

Lamb started planning right away. To save time and money, he did away with custom work wherever he could. But the architect knew he had other definite limits within which to work, including the building size, the site size, the money and time available, and zoning laws. These all had to be considered in the building's design.

Having committed to the project, those who called themselves Empire State, Inc., the development corporation, decided on the extent of the investment in the building itself. They estimated the cost of building one cubic foot, then concluded, using simple arithmetic, that the Empire State Building should be a structure of 36 million cubic feet.

But that wasn't the end of the pencil-pushing. They discovered that because of zoning laws, only about one-fourth of the two acres purchased could be built higher than 125 feet from the sidewalk without adding setbacks that would give the building a tiered effect.

Sixteen times, Lamb drew plans for Empire State. Fifteen times, changes were made in what was called the mythical topmost floor of the tower. Each time he redrew the plans, Lamb whittled away extraneous ells, wings, and buttresses in order to streamline the design.

The final plan, known as Plan K, was simple, based on the designs of the smaller steel-framed buildings that came before it. In other words, the design was unexceptional. The same steel frame, concrete floor slabs, and mechanical systems that made the building usable all were similar to those of other buildings. The only difference was the size of the structure.

"Plan K is Empire State," the planners wrote in 1931. "Five floors and five floors only, cover the whole area of the location

*The entrance itself stands four floors high, the spacious lobby, three... the base alone is an impressive building.*

[the base of the building]. The full set back requirements of the zoning law were applied, not as height made them incapable, but in one gorgeous gesture and at the height of only five floors from the street."[8]

Then, the sizes of the floors get smaller as the number of elevators decreases. The building's design consists of a pyramid of nonrentable space surrounded by a greater pyramid of rentable space.

With Plan K finally approved by the committee, a budget was fixed and several determinations made. First, no office space (once it was determined that the Empire State Building was to be an office building rather than a multipurpose unit) would be deeper than 28 feet, in order to take advantage of natural light from the outdoors. Next, as many stories of such space as possible would be built. The exterior would consist of limestone. Finally, the completion date would be May 1, 1931.[9]

Interestingly, Lamb designed the Empire State from the top down. Because the shape of the tower would determine the shape of the whole structure, the 86th floor was the first thing designed in order to ensure that elevator shafts, pillars, and foundation all went through from the top to the bottom of the building.

Early descriptions of the building are quite romantic:

*The entrance itself stands four floors high, the spacious lobby, three... the base alone is an impressive building. But at its roof, five floors above the street, there is a mighty terrace, sixty feet broad, which sweeps back to the foot of the tower. And from that point, separated from the surrounding buildings, to assure perpetual light and air, Empire State springs straight up to the sky. Uninterruptedly, the eye runs up the sides of Empire State from the fifth floor terrace to the 86th floor observatory.*[10]

However whimsical the building looked, the original plans had been based almost entirely on financial considerations, on standard real estate formulas, not on specific building plans or architectural design. In fact, Raskob's earliest reports to the developers did not contain drawings. The height of the building was decided by simply determining what height could be constructed with the money available, said William Starrett. The design and choice of construction materials was driven by function and by necessity.

The owners had required that construction be completed by May 1, 1931. As the contracts with Shreve, Lamb, and Harmon had been signed in September 1929 the builders had about twenty months to complete the building.

Other matters of concern required consideration, too. First, the elevator system. The mechanical engineer, Bassett Jones of Meyer, Strong, and Jones, emphasized the importance of collaboration from the earliest stages of design to avoid developing the building and steel plans without figuring in the elevators until afterward. Forgetting about the elevators in the Empire State would be the equivalent of forgetting to design the basement stairs to a house and finding you have to duck your head each time you go down to check the hot water heater—times one hundred!

*The vertical lines of polished steel begin at the sixth floor and extend upward for the full height, merging at the top in a great sunburst at the window heads.*

"The architectural, commercial, and popular success of the Empire State Building," wrote Edward W. Wolner in the *International Dictionary of Architects and Architecture*, "depended on a highly rationalized process, and equally efficient advertising and construction campaigns. Skillful designers of Manhattan office buildings, architects Shreve, Lamb, and Harmon were familiar with the imperatives of design and construction efficiency that maximized investors' returns by filling the building with tenants as soon as possible."

In addition, the New York Zoning Resolution of 1916 allowed unlimited building height but required several setbacks, "ziggurat-fashion," on the Empire State, intended to ensure that adequate daylight reached people on the street level of the city. "Coinciding as it did with New York's rise to commercial and cultural primacy, this simple rule changed the [stepped form] of the skyscraper as a type."[11]

### Icing the Cake

Architecture is said to be frozen music. The designers took it upon themselves to make the Empire State Building beautiful as well as practical. Style, the fashion of architecture, develops around how individual architects and other untrained builders put all of the pieces of line, shape, space, color, texture, and ornamentation together. Skyscraper style became a unique hodgepodge of European styles—Cubism, Russian Constructivism, and Italian Futurism—with abstraction, distortion, and simplification, particularly geometric shapes and highly intense colors, all celebrating the rise of commerce, technology, and speed.

This distinctive decorating style of the Empire State is known as Art Deco, which is a contraction of the name of the Exposition Internationale des Arts Décoratifs Industriels et Modernes, held in Paris in 1925. The term Art Deco didn't stick until the 1960s. When it was in fashion, it wasn't called Art Deco but rather modernistic or Style Moderne. Art Deco had indeed a heady, modern appeal. It became popular not only in architecture but also in jewelry, fashion, interior design, and, of course, furniture.

But "don't sell art deco short," admonishes Theodore James, who has written extensively about the Empire State Building and its décor. "It is more than high camp or current chic, more than tasseled cigarette cases and streamlined statuettes, more than a passing vogue for one in a series of sentimental stylistic revivals [like Middle Eastern, Greek,

*The distinctive Art Deco decoration style is most evident on the building's interior, where even the most functional item, such as the elevator, is a work of art.*

Roman, Egyptian, and even Mayan design]. It has come out of the closet (literally) to be legitimized as a bonafide subdivision of Style Moderne which dominated 20th century art for the '20s and '30s and also produced some of the most notable monuments of uniquely American construction."[12]

Some of the modern elements of Art Deco style are machine and automobile patterns and shapes such as stylized gears and wheels—also, at times, natural elements such as sunbursts and flowers. Nearly all of these elements are evident in the décor of the Empire State: the simple eagle heads flanking the Fifth Avenue entrance, the lacy, curlicue ceiling panels, the elevator doors and interiors, the metal bridge arching above the main lobby.

The special marble work in the ornamental panel facing the Fifth Avenue doorway should be noted. Between strips of bronze are marble inserts representing maps of New York and adjacent areas. A gauge registers the direction in which the wind is blowing at the top of the building, some 1,252 feet above.

Much of Empire State's interiors were designed by Rambush Studios, the same company that designed hundreds of ornate movie theaters in the 1920s and, later, the lobbies of the Waldorf-Astoria and Radio City Music Hall.

The lobby, two stories high, is faced with marble veined in dark blue and yellow; it is decorated with a narrow frame similar to the exterior of the main entrance. Behind the doorman's desk is an enormous aluminum and marble mural of the building.

The lobby's lighting is produced by concealed lamps that illuminate the circle and star motifs on the ceiling, which is decorated in platinum, gold, and aluminum leaf.

Two chrome steel bridges connecting either side of the mezzanine are designed to match the elevator doors.

Many of the offices were conservatively or traditionally decorated in all styles and tastes. However, despite the building's architectural style, Style Moderne was the least popular decorating approach. Tenants seemed to be more comfortable with the charming and decorative tried-and-true of the past rather than the sleek furnishings, chrome legs, and black lacquer tables of Art Deco.

Empire State's essential symbolic message, carved throughout the building's interior and its exterior in metal and concrete, is electrifying. It reminds the viewer of a dynamo's energy, of the power and promise of the Machine Age. This energy is also emblazoned on the Empire State's shimmering façade, the building's most distinguished architectural characteristic and perhaps its most functional, simply because the alloy plate used externally never tarnishes or dulls, even in salt air.

The façade is made of over 300 tons of chrome-nickel steel, which was also used for the window trim, mullions, and

Behind the doorman's desk is an enormous
Art Deco aluminum and marble mural
of the building.

*Name a skyscraper that looks as good today as it did 70 years ago, or one whose symbolism is undiminished...*

William Morgan

ornamental window heads. The building's construction notes stated, "The vertical lines of polished steel begin at the sixth floor and extend upward for the full height, merging at the top in a great sunburst at the window heads. It is again used in the mooring mast to the extent of 25 tons."[13]

Window openings are arranged in groups of twos and threes that are separated by limestone piers. Each window group is trimmed at the side with 10 inches of chrome-nickel steel, sandblasted to a velvety surface. The windows within each group are separated by double-width mullions of the alloy. These shiny plates blend perfectly with the window glass. Every glittering line points skyward and gives the appearance of "a soaring spire, rising from the base in an uninterrupted sweep, to the tower almost one fifth of a mile to the sky."[14]

The Empire State Building, looking quite like a chandelier in the New York sky, was designed toward the end of the Art Deco period, when skyscrapers were adorned with zigzagged appliqués.

Some experts feel the building's exterior lacks the raciness that was characteristic of the period and of the Art Deco style. This so-called lack of flamboyance in the building's style has at times been attributed to its principal architect, William Lamb, who was known for his somberness. Yet what some viewed as sobriety was perhaps in actuality a sophisticated mix of modern technology and classical principle, making the Empire State a "soaring, organic whole."[15]

"Name a skyscraper that has worn the test of time so well," challenges architectural historian William Morgan. The Empire State Building looks like a tall building should look. It gracefully comes to a peak, says Morgan, and it knows how to meet the sky. The changes at various levels with setbacks are vigorous, yet subtle and quite handsome. William Lamb, a serious architect with classical training, seemed to understand proportion and to realize that to be considered "good" at what one does doesn't require flamboyance, or newness for newness' sake.

"Name a skyscraper that looks as good today as it did 70 years ago, or one whose symbolism is undiminished," continues Morgan. Lamb was designing not to be flamboyant, but as the pyramid designers, or the designers of the Parthenon—he was designing for all ages.

Lamb produced a tall building like no other—superlative in all ways: as a functional piece of engineering, as architecture, as symbol. The design of the Empire State Building is a much stronger design than that of the Chrysler Building (which is fun for a while but is dated Deco rather than for-all-time Deco), far better than the Sears Tower in Chicago, the towers of the World Trade Center, and better even than the 1998 Petronas Towers of Kuala Lumpur, Malaysia, now the tallest in the world, peaking at an impressive 1,483 feet.

The setbacks on Empire State were given "a skillful buildup of scale at the lower levels, while the tower itself rises unflinchingly."[16] Indented setbacks in the center of each of the long sides help lateral scale. Another distinguishing feature was that it was one of the few skyscrapers with four façades, not just one facing the avenue. The shadows that so often come with deeply recessed windows and that mar the simple beauty of line were avoided in Empire State by setting the windows in thin metal frames, flush with the outer wall.

### The Finishing Touch

"It needs a hat!" Raskob reportedly said. It was decided that the "hat" would be used as a docking station for dirigibles, making the building 1,250 feet tall and bypassing the Chrysler Building, which was 1,046 feet tall. The plan was that a dirigible, or zeppelin, would be anchored to the mooring mast; passengers would disembark down a gangplank onto the 102nd floor. The dirigible could be serviced while it was docked at this location for three to four hours.

Only once did a dirigible dock at the mast, however. In September 1931, a small, privately owned dirigible made contact with the top of the building after half an hour of effort. Because of wind currents, it was able to stay moored for three minutes only. When the German dirigible *Hindenberg* exploded and burned over New Jersey a few years later, the idea for the mooring mast was quickly abandoned.

"We use skyscrapers and accept them as a matter of course," wrote William Starrett, "yet as each new one rears its head, towering among its neighbors, our sense of pride and appreciation is quickened anew and the metropolis takes it as its very own, and uncomplainingly endures the rattle and roar of its riveting hammers and the noises and the inconvenience of traffic which it brings. And this is because we recognize it as another of our distinctive triumphs, another token of our solid and material growth."[17]

And so we have it—the Empire State Building: A beloved icon of New York and America, that "mightiest peak of New York's mighty skyline," whose beauty lies not so much in its curb appeal as in its lofty heights, where "up there, among the clouds, the drumbeat of New York is stilled, the nervous staccato of the city's life is left behind. In the superb heights of the Empire State the mind is free. Here the real work which is the life blood of New York can be achieved restfully."[18]

*...up there, among the clouds, the drumbeat of New York is stilled, the nervous staccato of the city's life is left behind. In the superb heights of the Empire State the mind is free.*
William Starrett

*But New York's greatness is not in structure alone.*

*National Geographic Magazine*, November 1930

Chapter 2:
*The Workers: Classical Heroes in the Flesh*

*The Depression was terrible. People were livin' in cardboard boxes…
I seen people on the street beggin' for pennies, sellin' whatever they
could find—apples, a fountain pen, somethin' they picked up or stole.…
Basically they were honest people, but they stole to survive. They'd
steal clothin' off a rack on Orchard Street, pants, shirts, shoes.*

1930s New Yorker

*New York, ever a city of stark contrasts, boasted the tallest buildings, the most hungry people, and the longest unemployment lines at the very same time.*

Ask anyone who lived during the Depression in America, and they'll tell you stories that younger folks laugh at: "Oh sure, Mom and Dad, you walked ten miles to school and you shaved the dog to make blankets," we might tease. But for those who were alive in the 1930s, especially in the world's unofficial capital, New York, the joking wasn't that far from the truth.

One 1930s New Yorker said, "The Depression was terrible. People were livin' in cardboard boxes…I seen people on the street beggin' for pennies, sellin' whatever they could find— apples, a fountain pen, somethin' they picked up or stole….Basically they were honest people, but they stole to survive. They'd steal clothin' off a rack on Orchard Street, pants, shirts, shoes." [1]

While life wasn't quite as harsh for other Americans, many people found they had to rely once again on home gardens, canning, pickling, and baking. Meat was a once-in-a-while treat, while beans, pancakes, and macaroni and cheese were menu regulars. People started making their own clothes again, despite the fact that New York was the ready-made clothing capital of the world. Sometimes they lined a worn winter coat with old blanket material to make it do for another season.

But the so-called dirty thirties were more than just hard times. Perhaps even despite the hard times, people—ordinary people as well as those in leadership positions—seemed determined not to ask, "Is this all there is?"

The 1930s featured the contradictions of severe poverty and outlandish wealth. The first few years of the decade saw astonishing cultural changes create new markets. People had lived all their lives without electricity, let alone telephones. But by 1939, transatlantic flights, intercontinental phone calls, electric dishwashers, automobiles, synthetic materials, and even televisions had made their debut. Wonderful and still-stunning buildings were constructed; fanciful motion picture houses were erected all over the United States so Americans could enjoy extravagant Hollywood musicals.

While one-third of Americans lived below the poverty line, some industries actually managed to make a profit at the beginning of the 1930s as the person in the street looked for ways to escape from everyday drudgery. Thus, while the economy slumped, demand for cigarettes, movie tickets, gasoline, and other distractions increased. Social commentator Will Rogers joked, "We're the first nation in the history of the world to go to the poorhouse in an automobile." [2]

Some New Yorkers were somehow sheltered from the realities of the Depression altogether, as if they lived in a bubble. One woman claimed to have never seen a breadline except in newsreels, even though she had lived in the city throughout the Depression! Another said, "Even in Depression

*One of a host of organized protests marking the dissatisfaction of New Yorkers at the time of the Great Depression, when unemployment, soaring high school dropout rates, and homelessness were rife.*

A striking feature of 1930s New York was the contradiction of severe poverty and outlandish wealth. While many scraped a living, others had money to spare on luxuries such as flowers.

times, our neighborhood was very elegant. There…would be cabriolets like Hispano-Suizas, which was a very big foreign car, or an Isotto-Fraschine, which was very big, Brewsters, which were American-made Rolls-Royces, and the Minerva, another Spanish car. It was all 'veddy' fashionable." [3]

In some sectors, there was unbridled enthusiasm for what people and technology could do. With the same kind of devil-may-care speculation that had resulted in the stock market crash only months before, with general contracting at a near standstill and little or no work available, the announcement on August 29, 1929, about the planned construction of the Empire State Building was like a shout in the dark for the many willing workers who, affected by economic conditions, were standing in the unemployment lines or city breadlines. In the weeks to come, some of these workers would be employed, swarming around the building's skeleton as it fulfilled its destiny as New York's premier cloud tickler at record speed.

Passersby from every walk of life daily stopped to watch as construction workers nonchalantly crawled, walked, and swung on the 210 steel girders that formed the building's gigantic frame. While some may have wondered at the sanity of undertaking such an expensive task during such wobbly economic times, New Yorkers either instantly, or over time, expressed emotions such as love, awe, and pride for the Empire State Building.

**One Man's Journey**

On St. Patrick's Day, 1930, Ted Baron decided to go down to Fifth Avenue to watch the annual parade. He had arrived in New York City two years earlier, taking a Pilgrim Line[4] ship from New Bedford, Massachusetts, his hometown, to the New York docks. He was sixteen years old, the oldest of four children born of Polish immigrants.

Life in New York seemed gay and blithe to the casual observer. Soft lights, low music, sumptuous cafés, luxurious hotel lobbies, fashion parades on Fifth Avenue—a city that could tickle every fancy. Like so many others who came before him, New York City had beckoned to Ted as a place to which to escape, to find work, to send money home to his family in New Bedford, where the Depression was beginning to be felt, where jobs were scarce. Surely he could get a job in New York City, the biggest city in the world!

Ted's cousin Ziggy lived with his parents on the Lower East Side. From the docks, Ziggy took Ted on the nickel subway to their third-floor tenement flat. The Irish immigrants who arrived during the potato famine of the 1840s had first inhabited the area. As the Irish moved uptown, the Lower East Side tenements housed Italians, Jews, and Eastern Europeans.

*I'm looking around and all I see are fire escapes, fire escapes. Clothes hanging on fire escapes. Trash in the gutters. The smell, you know. Bare floors, no rugs…two days later, I was packing my bags, sneaking out of my aunt's apartment…she heard me walking across the floor and woke up…grabbed me by the arm, asked me where I was going? I'm going home, I told her. Give yourself some time, she said to me. Give yourself a couple of weeks to get used to it. Ziggy took me to Child's Restaurant hiring hall and I got a job. That was 1928. I worked for Child's for 26 years and became one of their youngest managers. But it took me three years to get used to living in New York City. I hated New York City.[5]*

What the casual visitor seldom saw in 1930 and perhaps even today were the 15-cent Bowery flops and the thinly clad, shivering men and women waiting in the early morning cold to grab the first papers on the street in order to search the help wanted columns for the chance at a job.

But Ted was one of the lucky ones who remained and prospered. He met his wife, Sophia Tylutka, known as Zo, a transplant from a small coal-mining town outside of Scranton, Pennsylvania. Zo had also migrated to New York City to find work and help her family. She was the eldest of nine children.

Zo hated being away from home. When Zo arrived in New York, she was as homesick as could be. She managed to find work as a governess and, later, as a companion to a single woman. But she was lonely, and it was a glad day when she ran into a friend from back home in the ladies' room of a Manhattan department store. The friend invited her to join her at a Young Democrats social club, where many members were of Polish descent, like Zo. One member of the club was Ted Baron, a young man with a charming smile and a well-cut suit (bought on Delancey Street) who liked to play cards and tell stories.

But on March 17, 1930, while Ted was spending his day off in usual fashion, looking for something to anchor him to this adopted city, something even more monumental was happening not far away. The ground was being broken for what would soon become the sky-puncturing Empire State Building.

*Here [in New York] obsolescence is a devil to be cast out and today's builder is tomorrow's vandal. You see the famous Waldorf-Astoria, where in its Turkish salon, the wealthy had once been served Turkish coffee by a "genuine Turk," turn to junk. Fountains of sparks hiss from its iron skeleton as clinging workmen wield their fiery cutting torches. And hard on the heels of its wreck comes the amazing Empire State Building.[6]*

Recalled Ted Baron,

*Where the Empire State Building is situated now there used to be a beautiful hotel…I think it was the Ritz Carlton [it was actually the Waldorf-Astoria] but I'm not too sure…and I lived on 25th and Second Avenue and I worked on 34th Street right off Sixth Avenue. And I saw them demolish this beautiful hotel and erect the Empire State Building. I walked back and forth six days a week….I remember looking through the knotholes they deliberately put there for what they called the "sidewalk superintendents." I saw all that heavy equipment….The Empire State Building has many cellars…4, 5, 6…I don't know…looking down there, they looked like toys. That's how deep it was. And they were driving them piles day and night, no stop. Boom boom boom, boom boom boom. More than one pile was going down at one time…they were more like cisterns…hollow…and they would keep on knocking them down until they hit bedrock…because Manhattan is one solid rock anyway…all these pipes…these pilings…different heights sticking up…then they would cut them all off even and they filled these huge things with reinforced concrete…so and that's what the Empire State Building is situated on. So I saw from the time they knocked it [the Waldorf-Astoria Hotel] down until they finished the Empire State Building.*

The existence of the first Waldorf-Astoria Hotel resulted from a feud and then a truce between two branches of the wealthy Astor family. William Waldorf Astor, great-grandson of John Jacob Astor, lived on the northwestern corner of Fifth Avenue and Thirty-third Street in a house inherited from his father, John Jacob Astor III. He planned to raze his house and on its site erect a hotel so tall that its shadow would fall on the residence of an aunt's home, a relative he detested. Mrs. Caroline Webster Chermerhorn Astor, the aunt in question, was unwilling to live in the midst of what she considered "sordid commercialism" and moved farther north on Fifth Avenue. Her son, John Jacob Astor IV, angered by his cousin's behavior, decided to tear down his mother's abandoned mansion and build a hotel even larger than the Waldorf. He named his hotel the Astoria after a trading post his great-grandfather had opened in Oregon. Eventually, dollar signs overcame the cousins' dislike for one another. They operated the two hotels as one, with the hyphenated name that became so famous, Waldorf-Astoria.

" 'Meet me at the Waldorf' became a byword among New York's elite 'Four Hundred'[7] during the Gay Nineties [1890s] and long afterward…at that location until 1929, when it was torn down to make way for the Empire State Building."[8]

Promptly following the first announcement of plans for the construction of the Empire State Building, a motor truck drove through the wide door of the Waldorf-Astoria—the door at which presidents and princes, rulers of state, and the uncrowned kings and queens of society had been received . The

*Actual demolition work on the Waldorf-Astoria Hotel, which was replaced by the Empire State Building, started on September 24, 1929, and all the masonry and steel was completely demolished to sidewalk level on February 3, 1930.*

truck, like a roaring invader, thrust its great bulk into the lobby where surely such an intruder never had been seen before. It churned across the floor, then turned and roared down "Peacock Alley," that proud corridor lined with gold mirrors and velvet drapes. The end of the old Waldorf had come.[9]

The former meeting place of the Four Hundred came to a rather unsophisticated end. Most of the building materials were unceremoniously carted away and loaded on barges. Five miles beyond Sandy Hook they were dumped into the ocean.

## Fateful Lessons

About the turn of the century, New York had been caught for a decade or more in fierce debate about whether the skyscraper was a good thing. At first, people living adjacent to the new skyscrapers of lower Manhattan often moved out in alarm. These high-rise buildings presented design and logistics problems that heretofore had not been addressed by architects or builders. High-rise buildings were viewed as dangerous. One had only to point to the tragedy of the Triangle Shirtwaist Company, considered the worst factory fire in the history of New York City, to revile the race to the sky.

On March 25, 1911, the Asch building, where the Triangle Shirtwaist Company employed five hundred women, mostly Jewish immigrants, on the top three of ten floors, caught fire. To keep the workers at their sewing machines, the proprietors had locked the doors leading to the exits. The fire began shortly after 4:30 P.M. in the cutting room on the eighth floor; fed by thousands of pounds of fabric, it spread rapidly.

Pump Engine Company No. 20 and Ladder Company No. 20 arrived quickly, but their ladders extended only to the sixth floor. To add to the tragedy, life nets broke when the women jumped from the roof in groups of three and four. One hundred and forty-six women died in less than 15 minutes. The owners of the company were charged with manslaughter. They were later acquitted, but in 1914 were ordered by a judge to pay damages of $75 each to the families of the 23 victims who had sued.

While the Triangle Shirtwaist Company tragedy focused public attention on labor issues such as working conditions as well as on firefighting efficiency, it was also a reminder of the dangers of tall buildings that one could not get quickly into and out of. Advances in invention, such as the development of the elevator by Elisha Otis for gaining access and exit to upper building floors and the use of steel frames to support the massive weight of a building, overcame these earlier obstacles, and the sky itself became the limit for architects and engineers to conquer.

## American Manpower

Manhattan's skyscrapers came to symbolize the modern city. Yet, surprisingly, they were built in part by New York's oldest residents. In the 19th century, Caughnawaga Indians who were employed as ironworkers developed a reputation for fearlessness and adeptness at walking on high steel.

The Native American penchant for what became known as "skywalking" was partly a response to the unfair labor conditions they encountered. But it became a rite of passage for young men to follow in their fathers' and grandfathers' footsteps, high into the clouds of New York.

Following the Civil War era, in 1886, the Dominion Bridge Company set out to build a bridge over the St. Lawrence River for the Canadian Pacific Railroad. They planned to anchor the bridge on land belonging to the Kahnawake Mohawks. In exchange, because in the 1800s there were few opportunities for Native Americans to earn wages comparable to whites, the Mohawks wanted jobs on the project. The company's expectations were low, but to their surprise the workers were all over the bridge, climbing with agility and without the slightest fear of dangerous heights.

Pleasantly astonished, the company trained the workers in the difficult task of riveting, a dangerous skill that entailed heating rivets until they were red-hot, tossing them 30 to 40 feet through the air, then catching and forcing them through steel beams with a hammer or a pneumatic drill—all of this some 500 feet or more above the ground. Mohawk crews soon were working all over the Northeast as word spread of their natural and acquired construction skills.[10]

About 1915, a Caughnawaga Mohawk named John Diablo traveled to New York City and got work on the Hell Gate Bridge crossing the East River. One day he unfortunately lost his footing, fell into the East River, and drowned. His work companions took his body back to the reservation near Montreal, Quebec, and nothing more was heard of the Caughnawaga in New York until 1926, when they were attracted by the great construction boom that was resulting in buildings like the Chrysler and the Empire State. Working hundreds of feet in the air—on girders narrower than a diving board—tradition led thousands of Caughnawagas to hammer, drill, and weld the New York skyline into being. They were joined by New York's latest residents, newly arrived immigrants, who had once, like Polish immigrant Ted Baron, looked up from the streets in wonder at Manhattan's towers.

The ironworkers rode the girders as they were swung into position so they could slip bolts into place temporarily until the bolter came along to tighten them. These men worked in the most exposed places, but passersby were entranced as they

*An army of workers was deployed at the Empire State construction site, digging and setting foundations, and fabricating and milling columns and beams, using some 57,000 tons of steel. They laid 10 million bricks, poured 62,000 cubic yards of cement, set 6,400 windows, and installed seven miles of elevator shafts for 63 elevators.*

The "gunman" of this riveting gang hangs
precariously in midair, relying on a wooden
plank to support him as the bucker-up helps
hold the rivet in place.

nonchalantly handled tools and waved directions to the derrick crews with not even a safety belt in sight.

The riveters worked in teams of four: the heater (passer), the catcher, the bucker-up, and the gunman. The heater placed about ten rivets into the fiery forge. When they were red-hot, he used a pair of three-foot tongs to toss them one by one to the catcher, who was often 50 to 75 feet overhead.

The catcher used an old paint can to catch the still-glowing rivet. With his other hand, he removed the rivet from the can with tongs, knocked the cinders off, then placed the rivet in one of the holes in a beam.

The bucker-up rigged a flimsy contraption of planks so that he could actually be in space to do his job, which involved neither standing nor sitting but squatting in a posture most of us would need a heating pad to correct that evening. In that strange position, he held the rivet while the gunman used a riveting hammer (powered by compressed air) to push it into the girder.

A safety man could usually be observed crawling up the outside of the Empire State scaffolding to check for loose planks, stray wires, and forgotten tools that might drop to the street and crown an innocent sidewalk superintendent.

These men worked all the way from the street to the 102nd floor, over a thousand feet up. At lunchtime on a cold day, they toasted their sandwiches on the rivet forge.

### Captured on Film

Some of these construction workers—walking, squatting, and sitting where no creature but a seagull ought to be—appear in the brilliant photographs of Lewis Hine, who had lived in the late 1800s depression in Wisconsin. When the factories closed, Hine made do with odd jobs like cutting firewood and acting as a delivery boy. In the early 1900s, he came into contact with social welfare organizations and began making photo studies of life in the slums, of child labor, and of the activities of the Red Cross during World War I, "documenting the dark side of the great American dream."[11] According to his résumé, in 1930 Hine was hired as staff photographer by the Empire State

Corporation to document the manpower involved in building the skyscraper from start to finish.

In a letter dated November 25, 1930, Hine wrote:

*My six months of skyscraping have culminated in a few extra thrills and finally achieving a record of the Highest Up when I was pushed and pulled onto the Peak of the Empire State, the highest point yet reached on a man-made structure. The day before, just before the high derrick was taken down, they swung me out in a box from the hundredth floor (a sheer drop of nearly a quarter of a mile) to get some shots of the tower... I have always avoided dare-devil exploits and do not consider these experiences, with the cooperation the men have given me, as going quite that far, but they have given a new zest of high adventure and perhaps, a different note in my interpretation of Industry.*[12]

Hine's photographs, as well as the drawings of his contemporary, Vernon Howe Bailey, have preserved forever the accomplishment of these craftsmen, the majority of them nameless to those of us who have come after. Their skill and energy made possible the building of the Empire State.

*...just before the high derrick was taken down, they swung me out in a box from the hundredth floor (a sheer drop of nearly a quarter of a mile) to get some shots of the tower...*

Lewis Hine

*Grand Central Station, built in 1913 and recently extensively remodeled. It combines the romance of train travel and the history of a bygone era.*

## Purple

By Roland Maycock

Park Avenue
The roof the Grand Central Building hanging
like a chandelier of opaque, yellow glass
against a ceiling draped with blue velvet

A cold, clear night

patches of snow and ice chequered against the
black pavement

Floors of black and white marble

A sharp, cold breeze scurries around a corner
She draws the collar of her fur coat against her
cheeks she laughs

The exotic, mask-like face on the Corday
perfume advertisement

The sharp click of high heels against the side
walk on a quiet night

she says something about snow and moonlight

she says it because she is like snow and
moonlight with eyes of black onyx

And her words are like attenuated music
because I think of roses and ivory with eyes of
star dust and dew

Words are spoken

words, minor thirds on a green Steinway piano
with pastel peonies painted on it

Broadway
a brocatelle of lights and color

a potpourri of sounds and surging people
surging, surging, fat play-boys splurging, gaiety
verging

on hysteria

Glamour

Whoopee

Silken hose, twinkling slippers, daffodil hair
and purple, pansy eyes

Banjos throbbing, drums insinuating a
syncopating beat, saxophones wailing like
unicorns lost in a green fog

Laughs, tinkling of piano keys beneath darting
finger tips

She says something about the music and hums
a snatch of the tune as we dance

She talks about the music because she likes it
and is like it, it and the raspberry lipstick that
curves her lips into an enticing bow

And her words are lost as the music leaps from
a capricious softness to a blaring crescendo.

The park
whispers of spring fill the air that has forgotten
the threnodies of autumn

The arching span of a stone bridge

And across the surface of the water the images
of trees ripple, blending their virgin green with
the reflected gold of the tower of the Sherry
Netherland hotel

Dreams come like the sound of a violin
pastorale that echoes through arcades of
blossoming trees

Haunting, remembering through the park

The starless void of a dark sky and a sea that
undulates and gleams with phosphorous

Lagoons, wine red at sunset

lagoons, pearl moons and silver

The constant hum of autos purring

spoons in a Chop Suey restaurant on Broadway

Wide blue eyes, luminous

questioning and being questioned; wondering
and wondered at

a voice as low as muted silver harps and soft
as satin

Something that teases, catches and remembers
a slim, blue book of poetry by Conrad Aiken

reading:

Clearly you sound to me in the night-time,
Solemnly, like a rich wind moving,

You move in my heart's enchanted forest;

You sigh and are restless.[13]

# Blood

By Leonard A. Hoffman

Broadway
a swirling mob
The sun streaming down in all its brilliance
Jazz tunes floating out from music stores
A well dressed youth loitering near a drug
store, suddenly clenches his fists
sliding with a moan to the pavement.

Large crimson drops ooze sluggishly from
between his clenched fingers
after tracing a scarlet line upon his taut flesh,
fall reluctantly to the sidewalk.

Oblivious to the morbid crowd which gathers
around him, the youth stares at the fantastic
designs traced upon the street by his life
blood…His hands, wallowing in the crimson
channel, never once relinquish their grasp
upon the wound…The murmuring of the
crowd increases…a policeman makes his way
to the side of the stricken youth.
*"So, they gottcha at last, eh, Jerry?"*
*"Yeah,"* groans the youth.

The wail of a siren pierces the air
an ambulance plows its way through the
heavy traffic
White-dressed men with poker faces gently lift
the wounded boy into the ambulance
again the shriek of the siren and the traffic
ceases temporarily.

The spectacle is over
but the crowd still stares in breathless wonder
at the blood-stained pavement.

*"Paper, Mister?"* cries an urchin in tattered
clothes and dirt streaked face as he wends his
way through the crowd, proffering his Dailies
to the spectators
This is sacrilege
The crowd is shocked
Men shake their heads, and the noisy intruder
slinks away disappointed.

A man with a derby tilted on his head now
approaches the center of the mass
He opens a heavy black bag. With a few quick
manipulations, he creates a stand on which silk
ties are exposed.

*"Here y'are, gents,"* touts the slick salesman.
*"Silk ties jest to advertise sold at half cost. Step closer,
gents, and let me demonstrate…."*

Slowly the crowd drifts over to watch the
new display
The group is interested
here is another performance to witness.

A flabby man with hanging jowls emerges
from the drugstore
Undaunted by the fierce glances cast in his
direction by the few stragglers, he proceeds
to obliterate the crimson stains
When this task is accomplished, the sturdy
man waddles back to the store
The few staunch spectators move on
the final scene of the big show is ended
Broadway[14]

## Shades

By Paul J. Elkin

Walked down the elevated steps.
And reached the level of the street.
I saw men hurrying home with papers
And women carrying bundles.
I noticed boys without hats
And aged telegraph messengers.
I heard a man hawking bananas
From a cart, at three for a nickel.
I saw a mother slap her three year old
Child, and I should have interfered.
I didn't because she would have told me
To mind my own business.
Another woman, footsore and forlorn,
Laboriously pushed a baby coach.
I would offer to assist her.
She would say "Fresh!"
Women are like that.
I saw one man buy "The Sun"
And another "The Graphic."
And they looked the same to me.
I went down into the subway.
A fat woman was changing a quarter
And dropped three nickels.
No one helped her pick them up.
Two boys tried to
Squeeze through on one fare,
And were promptly
Apprehended by a man
Who wore spats and derby.
One boy cried, but
The other was defiant.
I would have offered the change
But the man would say
"No, you're only encouraging them."
Two over-rouged girls enter.
They wear leather boots and
Shabby fur coats.
They wink at every man.
They work in Macy's.

In the train, women with
Babies stand, while
Men with newspapers sit.
One woman out of ten
Says "Thank you" when
A seat is given her.
The local is crowded.
The express is suffocating.
It's six o'clock.
Everyone's going home.[15]

*Here no one can say how soon any structure may vanish.*[1]

Frederick Simpich

# Chapter 3:
## *The Construction Schedule*

## Cha-ching!

The city kept growing. No sooner was a building built, it seemed, than it was sold quickly at auction, torn down, and replaced. In such a competitive atmosphere, combined with the severe economic slump, developers wanted to ensure that the Empire State Building won the race to the skies and to meet the "inexorable demands of finance."[2] After all, office space couldn't be rented until the building was complete.

So-called fast-track construction, an innovation in 1930 (yet common today in about 40 percent of construction projects), compresses the project schedule by running design and construction phases simultaneously. For example, in a typical fast-track project, foundation and steel packages are purchased before the building layout is fixed. Time is money. Therefore, design may run as little as a week ahead of construction, and myriad design decisions are made in the field.

Because the final costs are generally unknown during the process, the potential for profit, from the commercial developers' point of view, is worth the risk. The construction managers may have to buy materials at slightly inflated prices, but by saving time, they hope to make up the cost on the interest on the construction loan and on rent collections.

Present-day construction companies, engineers, and developers can only imagine what it was like to undertake a project as big as the Empire State Building… Place yourself in an office in lower Manhattan in September 1929 when Pierre du Pont dropped in and said, "I need your help to build the world's tallest building." Where would you start? Terence V. Milholland, Executive Vice President of EDS Corporation, breaks it down in a speech to colleagues delivered in 2001:

*First step—Demolish the large hotel sitting on the site. Next—Hire thousands of contractors, including hundreds of Mohawk Indians who, unafraid of heights, can rivet giant steel beams together with great agility. Then arrange for the milling and transportation of 57,000 tons of steel from Pennsylvania. Every morning, steel suppliers lined up on the New Jersey side of the Hudson River, ready to send new beams across the water and up 34th Street at the moment they're needed.*

*Your project team orders 10 million bricks, 62 thousand cubic yards of concrete and 6,400 windows. And when they are done, just 20 [sic] months later, they've built the world's tallest building, the Empire State Building.*

This historic feat shows us "deliverables" from great project managers—requiring hard work, planning, coordination, and recruitment and encouragement of skilled workers. And all were done without help from computers and software.

While only in business since 1925, some four years before landing the Empire State Building contract, but with a combined 35 years in the building business, Starrett Brothers and Eken was the company chosen to head the construction of

*An early panorama looking south from Radio City prior to the building of the World Trade Center in 1972. Today the skyline is again empty of those structures.*

the Empire State Building. It was a good choice, considering the company's accomplishments with respect to time and precision. As its current company profile points out, Starrett still prides itself on these achievements today:

*The foundation of Starrett's success is our long history in the acquisition and development of real estate. Time and again, we have proven our ability to complete complex commercial and residential projects in urban settings throughout the world. For example, Livingston Plaza in downtown Brooklyn, the 550,000 square foot headquarters for the Metropolitan Transit Authority, was completed in 16 months and Manhattan Park on Roosevelt Island, a 1,100 unit residential complex, was built in a remarkable 13 months.*

*These accomplishments are made possible by the creativity and flexibility of an experienced management team. We approach each project with an owner's perspective and commit ourselves to finishing on time and under budget…Our developments visually and culturally enhance their surroundings while benefiting from the unique Starrett touch.*[3]

As part of the bid to get the job, Paul Starrett bet on a long shot and won. Instead of saying that he had everything necessary to build the Empire State in the required time, Starrett took an opposite stance. When asked how much equipment his company had on hand, Starrett got the developers' attention when he said his company didn't even have a pick and shovel.

With his foot in the door, Starrett went on to explain that the Empire State was no ordinary building and was going to present unusual challenges. Ordinary building equipment wouldn't cut it. Rather than renting expensive equipment, his idea was to buy new equipment specifically fitted for the job at hand. Once the job was completed, the equipment would be sold and the proceeds credited to the developers.

A team/committee approach accompanied by the employment of subcontractors considered experts in their areas of specialization was used in the design, planning, and construction of the Empire State Building.

In an effort to avoid duplication of effort and loss of time on the project, the committee consisted of the owners, architects, and builders. Given this organic organizational method, everyone knew exactly and approved each step of the process. From the moment they began meeting, group members worked simultaneously on both immediate and future deadlines. It was really an extraordinary accomplishment, an outstanding example of the power of coordinated effort.

**Demolishing the Old to Make Way for the New**
The demolition of the Waldorf-Astoria began just two days after the contract with Starrett Brothers was signed.

In 1890, William Waldorf Astor had decided to raze the family mansion on the corner of Fifth Avenue and Thirty-third Street and build the largest, most luxurious hotel in the world. The 13-story Waldorf Hotel opened in 1893 and was instantly the talk of the town. Its success inspired John Jacob Astor,

William's cousin, who owned the other half of the block, to demolish his house and build an adjacent connected hotel. The Astoria was combined with the Waldorf in 1897 to form the Waldorf-Astoria. Over the years, New York's fashionable society gathered, dined, and was entertained in its public rooms.

But 30 short years later, the destruction of the Waldorf-Astoria was complete, down to the last stone buried below the old foundations. Demolition took less than five months.

Meanwhile, orders went out for steel, cement, lime, marble, lumber, hardware, and more. The engineering firm of Post and McCord prepared the steel skeleton of Empire State—60,000 tons of structural steelwork.

With the hotel dismantled and its remains either dumped in the ocean or salvaged for other uses, the next army of workers was deployed at the site.

*Thirty years after it was opened, the Waldorf-Astoria complex was summarily dismantled and its remains either dumped in the ocean or salvaged for other uses.*

In their pursuit of speed, the builders kept contact between the various trades to a minimum. Because each trade operated at its own speed, this cut down on the risk of delays that could topple the entire project like a domino effect.

On-site concrete mixing prevented the potential delays resulting from cement trucks jostling Manhattan traffic. The use of material hoists, passenger elevators, and the railroad was coordinated and controlled throughout the site, keeping the huge subcontracting system running smoothly.

Over 60 trades had to be represented among those hired to work on the Empire State Building. Supplies had to be ordered to exact specifications, and the timing of their arrival had to be precise.

Even if you are unfamiliar with carpentry and construction, the following highlights will make you appreciate the monumental effort necessary to acquire and distribute the materials needed to build a structure as massive as the Empire State Building.

When the architect's design was approved, calls immediately went out for materials. Requisitions were given to the steel mills in Pittsburgh. Cement and lime were ordered from upstate New York. Indiana quarrymen began the tough, dusty job of cutting stone. Marble was harvested from Germany and France. Loggers reaped lumber from the Pacific coast. Hardware was fashioned in New England's factories. Every order was exact and complete, specifying quantity, size, length, weight, and precise date of delivery.

Everything about the Empire State Building was designed to expedite its construction. Prefabricated material was used as much as possible. These preassembled wares, including structural steel, chrome and nickel trims, steel window frames, and aluminum spandrels, floor arches, and outside walls, allowed speedy framework construction and the rapid installation of hundreds of internal items that followed—plumbing, heating, ventilation, electrical work, elevators, marble works, and interior finishes of all sorts. As a result, work progressed at a rate of about four stories each week. The entire framework took only 23 weeks to erect.

The Art Deco style of the Empire State Building required lush surface materials for its completion. The building's exterior is a combination of 200,000 cubic feet of Indiana limestone and granite and 10 million common bricks, trimmed with glossy aluminum and chrome-nickel steel from the sixth floor to the top. The ceiling of the lobby features polished marble imported from France, Italy, Belgium, and Germany.

The walls of all entrance halls, corridors, and elevator lobbies have a base course of Belgian black marble. Above this base, all the pilasters, door trim, and panels throughout are finished in Est Rellante and Formosa Rose marble from

*Everything about Empire State was designed for expediency. Wherever possible, prefabricated materials were used to allow for rapid installation.*

Germany. These marbles are also used on the stairways leading from the first to the second floor and also for the stairways from the first floor to the basement, with treads of Travertine marble from Italy. The floors of all the entrances, lobbies, and corridors throughout are furnished in Belgian blue Belge marble for the borders with the field of Red Levanto marble from Italy and Bois Jordan marble from France.

It was particularly difficult to obtain the harmony of colors required by the architect, and a special envoy was sent to Europe and to the quarries to ensure that the marble would be exact in color and sent on time. The task of cutting the marble fell to craftsmen like Nick Acson, a native of Kyuthia, Turkey. The marblework at the Empire State Building was one of his first jobs in the United States.

To get some sense of the immensity of just one aspect of this project, consider the marble inserts in the ornamental panel that faces the Fifth Avenue doorway. In order to create the inserts, which depict maps of New York and adjacent territories, 80 patterns for the marble had to be cut to size just to depict the shoreline of Long Island! But few people, including Nick Acson, thought twice about the difficulty of the work or the prestige of working on the world's tallest skyscraper. For old-world craftsmen of the Depression era, pride in one's work came in the form of a job completed and well done, resulting in food on the family table and the reputation it took to land the next job. Acson returned to his native Turkey after working in the New York area, where he died a relatively young man, too soon to tell his children his tales of helping to construct the world's most famous building.

**Prepping the Site**

Had all the materials used to build the Empire State been delivered at once, a train 57 miles long would have been needed! While the locomotive would be stationed in New York, the caboose would still be located in Bridgeport, Connecticut!

With ordered material on its scheduled way to the building site, the task of organizing the building plant and equipment was at hand. Job preparation is perhaps tiresome and often seems as if it takes twice as long as the actual construction. Compare the relatively simple work of prepping one room in a house just for new trim, paint, and wallpaper. Most mortals can't fathom what "prep work" really meant for the Empire State construction crews.

Once the foundations were in place but before actual construction began, temporary passenger elevators and open-car mine cage passenger hoists, material hoists, concrete and mortar mixing machinery for floor arches, and basement and

EMPIRE STATE
CRAFTSMANSHIP AWARDS

| | |
|---|---|
| GEORGE R. ADAMS | PAINTER AND DECORATOR |
| ADAM BIGELOW | DAMP PROOFER |
| GUS COMEDECA | STEAM SHOVEL OPERATOR |
| JOHN CONNOLLY | ROOFER |
| WILLIAM DENEEN | ELEVATOR CONSTR'S HELPER |
| LOUIS HUMMELL | STEAMFITTER |
| JAMES IRONS | STONE CUTTER |
| ARTHUR JONES | ORN. IRON & BRONZE WORKER |
| JAMES P. KERR | STONE SETTER |
| FRANK J. KLEIN | PLASTERER |
| VLADIMIR KOZLOFF | WRECKER |
| SAMUEL LAGINSKY | GLAZIER |
| JOSEPH LEFFERT | TILE SETTER'S HELPER |
| PETER MADDEN | ASBESTOS WORKER |
| R. MADDALENA | TILE SETTER |
| FERRUCCIO MARIUTTO | TERRAZZO WORKER |
| MATTHEW M. McKEAN | CARPENTER |
| THOMAS McWEENEY | ELEVATOR CONSTRUCTOR |
| FRANK MOEGLIN | SHEET METAL WORKER |
| WILLIAM L. MORAN | STEAM FITTER'S HELPER |
| JOHN E. O'CONNOR | PLUMBER |
| FRANK W. PIERSON, JR. | METAL LATHER |
| GUISEPPE RUSCIANI | LABORER |
| GINO SANTONI | CEMENT MASON |
| OWEN SCANLON | MARBLE SETTER'S HELPER |
| CHARLES E. SEXTON | BRICKLAYER |
| LOUIS SHANE, JR. | MARBLE SETTER |
| CLIFFORD SMITH | ELECTRICIAN |
| MICHAEL TIERNEY | ROCK DRILLER |
| PIETRO VESCOVI | TERRAZZO WORKER'S HELPER |
| THOMAS F. WALSH | HOISTING ENGINEER |
| THOMAS WALSH | DERRICKMAN |

*This plaque celebrating the work and professionalism of some of the 3,400 people involved in the construction of Empire State resides in the lobby of the building.*

*Workers from over 60 trades were hired for the construction of the Empire State Building. Here, a worker operates one of the many cranes used to move the most cumbersome of building materials. Smaller lifts, a railroad, and even hand carts were also used to move items.*

The building is supported by 210 columns all braced in each direction on the center line. For wind bracing a design pressure of 20 pounds per square foot was used above the sixth floor and 30 pounds per square foot above the 86th floor.

sub-basement floors all had to be constructed and installed. The temporary elevators lifted fast and ran roughly, carrying large numbers of laborers to their workstations.

When observing the building's construction from the street, sidewalk superintendents saw "a forest of derricks and columns with naked skeleton construction that in a few hours changed form and grew into a monumental structure." [4]

"A perfect timetable was published each morning. At every minute of the day builders knew what material was going up on each of the elevators, to which height it would rise, and which gang of workers would use it." [5]

Steel structural beams arrived as they were needed. Just 80 hours elapsed between their birth in the rolling mills and their installation—while still warm—in the framework. For structural engineers H. G. Balcom and Associates, the main challenge was designing the steel frame to meet wind loads. The building is supported by 210 columns with a maximum cross section of 640 square inches. Nearly all columns are braced in each direction on the center line, and deep knee braces at service areas are concentrated in the core of the building. For wind bracing, a design pressure of 20 pounds per square foot was used above the 6th floor and 30 pounds per square foot above the 86th floor. [6]

*Meant to be the tallest structure on earth, the Empire State Building was considered in 1930 to be the largest commercial venture and investment ever. Today, with 2,248,369 square feet of space, it houses over one thousand businesses and has its own ZIP code.*

*This worker helps guide a hoist used to move large steel beams, heavy machinery, and more into place at the Empire State construction site.*

An overhead monorail trolley system was built for unloading materials on the main floor, and an entire railway system ran throughout the construction site for distributing materials. An interior hoisting system was employed because of the large floor area—about 425 feet by 197 feet. This approach was cheaper than exterior steel hoist shafts installed outside the building would have been.

Stone erection equipment, steel guy derricks for lifting heavy machinery, and saw rigs and filing machines also had to be raised into place. All limestone slabs from the 6th floor setback to the 86th-floor roof were cut in precise sizes that could be raised easily by the material hoists. Practically everything except the structural steel and a few large machinery units was raised on these hoists, utilizing six 200-horsepower hoisting engines, two concrete buckets, and four steel platform cages.

Two additional relay hoists used to hoist material between the 77th and 86th floors also served the mooring mast construction above the 86th-floor level.

The concrete mixing plant for floor arch construction consisted of two ¾-yard capacity mixers on skids, each equipped with 15-horsepower motors. Four other ¾-yard concrete mixers were used for pouring basement walls and supplementing the concrete floor arch units on the large floor areas. A small, portable, gasoline-driven mixer was also used for pouring concrete for fireproofing.

To unload stone from trucks inside the building, four sections of overhead monorail or trolley were installed with a working load of 8,000 pounds. Most of the exterior limestone was unloaded by this system and trucked on flat cars to the inside hoists for distribution to work areas throughout the building.

An industrial railway system was constructed inside the building for distributing materials. Each car in this 12-gauge railway weighed approximately 1,150 pounds; 24 platform cars had a capacity of two to three tons, while smaller carts on wheels were utilized for minor distributing tasks.

Stone erection equipment consisted of 30 hand-powered winches with a capacity for 1,200 pounds of lift for setting stone in all stories above the setback at the 6th floor. This stone, too, was raised by the inside material hoists, except for stones at the top of the building that were large enough to be lifted by a steel erection derrick located on the 86th-floor roof.

Post and McCord, the steel erectors, had their own erection derricks in use, but an additional 15-ton derrick was placed on the 6th-floor setback roof on the Thirty-fourth Street side of the building. Another slightly smaller derrick was placed at the 25th-floor setback roof. These derricks were used to hoist form

*An industrial railway system was constructed inside the building for distributing materials. Each car in this 12-gauge railway weighed approximately 1,150 pounds; 24 platform cars had a capacity of two to three tons, while smaller carts on wheels were utilized for minor distributing tasks.*

*Ironworkers, many of them Caughnawaga Mohawks, became known as "skywalkers" as they rode the girders high above the city streets.*

lumber for concrete floor arches and machinery too large for the material hoists. In addition to the heavy equipment, a host of electric saws, band saws, and crosscut saws was also used.

A steel plate chute to catch dirt and refuse was constructed instead of the standard wooden chute commonly installed for such purposes. It was decided that the steel plate chute would wear better and could even be sold after construction was completed. Workers used small wheelbarrows to roll debris to the chutes.

To save money on overtime paid to the elevator construction crew that was working on the 63 permanent elevators, some other way to get the men to their workstations had to be rigged. "To avoid the payment of this excess time and to give the elevator constructors unobstructed use of all the permanent shafts, it was decided to install an absolutely independent system of temporary elevators to take care of passenger service during the construction period," said the construction notes.

An erection gang was steadily employed to carry out the elevator installations as the steel erection work progressed, allowing the men to ride farther and farther up to their eagle's nest–high work spots.

Two mine cage lifts were installed as soon as the steel erection permitted. The first went from the 1st to the 10th floor. When steel was erected to the 21st floor, the second lift went as high as the 20th floor. These passenger cages were built for a load of 3,500 pounds and were enclosed on three sides.

Elevator operators on the cars signaled machine rooms using colored lights to indicate the direction of travel required and floors on which they needed to stop. "These units were the most flexible to use for quick installation to take care of the daily increasing demands for raising 2,803 men to a reasonable height below the rapidly mounting steel structure, which ultimately [reached] an erection record of one story per day."

Four elevator units that had been salvaged from the demolition of the Waldorf-Astoria Hotel were also installed for temporary use during construction. With two additional Otis Elevator cars running from the sub-basement to the 25th floor and two more from the ground floor to the 43rd, all the needs for passenger service during the construction period were met.

**Distributing the Building Material**
All material except the structural steel was received and unloaded at one of the seven entrances (four on the Thirty-fourth Street side and three on the Thirty-third Street side) on the main floor of the building.

Driveways about 25 feet wide extended around the four sides of the main floor. Trucks could drive completely around

*All material except the structural steel was received and unloaded at one of the seven entrances (four on Thirty-fourth Street and three on Thirty-third Street) on the main floor of the building.*

The steel tonnage in the Empire State Building
exceeded at that time by a large margin the
amount used in any comparable structure. For
example, the Chrysler Building utilized
21,000 tons and the Manhattan Company
Building used 18,500 tons.

the building with enough room to pass one another as they unloaded and handled some 500 loads of various kinds of materials, machinery, and equipment (not counting the structural steel) during a typical eight-hour workday.

**Structural Steel—57,480 Tons of It**

The steel tonnage in the Empire State Building exceeded at that time by a large margin the amount used in any comparable structure. For example, the Chrysler Building utilized 21,000 tons and the Manhattan Company building used 18,500 tons.

The first steel columns were set on April 7, 1930, and the building had to be completed and ready for occupancy by May 1, 1931. It took 350 men to do the job of setting the columns. In fact, four main divisions of the construction work set the pace for those that followed: structure steel erection, concrete floor arch construction, exterior metal trim and aluminum spandrels and windows, and exterior limestone.

The contractors, Post and McCord, had from April to October to get the steel erected, and 80 percent was in place by August 1. It was claimed that during July, 22 stories of steel were placed in as many working days, with only regular hours, no night work, and a five-day workweek throughout the period.

The steel was shipped from the shops (made by Carnegie Steel Company and fabricated by American Bridge Company and the McClintic-Marshall Company, subsidiaries of United States Steel Corporation) as fast as it was fabricated and stored in the Pennsylvania Railroad yards in Greenville, New Jersey (near Bayonne). From there, the steel was lightered to the East River waterfront and trucked to the construction site as required. Alternate sections from the basement to the roof, comprising from two to eight floors each, were assigned to each fabricator. The required steel was ordered one lift (two floors) at a time. Because no storage space was available at the building site, it was necessary that everyone be ready to erect the steel when it arrived. "The largest shipping pieces were the two bottom column sections, the lower one 15 feet 8 inches long, weighing 44 tons and the upper one having about the same weight but being 33 feet long," wrote the *Engineering News Record* in August 1930.

**Concrete—62,000 Cubic Yards of It**

The floors for 85 stories, including the main roof, were completely poured on October 6, 1930, only days after the structural steel was completely set and four days ahead of schedule. Throughout the main building, four-inch cinder concrete floor arches were used, reinforced with galvanized welded fabric. Over 62,000 cubic yards of concrete were placed in these arches.

Workers wheeled buggies with a capacity of six cubic yards that held enough cement to create 12 to 15 square feet of floor. Several other men would stand in the wet concrete and spread

*Four main divisions of the construction work set the pace for those that followed: structure steel erection, concrete floor arch construction, exterior metal trim and aluminum spandrels and windows, and exterior limestone.*

*Workers not only contended with dizzying heights, but also with hefting heavy materials like huge blocks of Indiana limestone into place.*

*Those employed in the construction of the
Empire State Building no doubt considered
themselves lucky to be in work, because in
1930, American workers lost between two and
a half and three billion dollars in wages in four
months alone.*

*Window openings were designed in groups of two and three, separated by limestone piers, and trimmed with chrome-nickel steel, allowing maximum natural light in the interior and offering an uninterrupted glittering exterior line.*

it into position, pushing it into the wooden forms around the beams to create beam encasements. Workers constantly had to mix the concrete by hand to keep the cement from rising to the top and the aggregate from settling to the bottom. As soon as a concrete slab was complete, tracks were laid on it for a miniature industrial railway used during the entire construction process.

### Bricks—10 Million of Them

Besides the four leading divisions in the construction, the builders had to address the receiving and distribution of the 10 million common bricks, 800,000 face bricks, and nearly two million terra-cotta tiles used on the Empire State. The methodology used was considered a distinct innovation for a building operation of that type.

Because of their fragility, the terra-cotta tiles (used for interior partitions around permanent elevator shafts) were unloaded by hand and stacked along railway spurs from which they could be quickly hoisted to appropriate floors. There, masons laid the tiles in the same way as brick. The problem was to raise the bricks fast enough to keep pace with the stone setting and adhere to the goal of at least one story enclosed per day.

"It is no exaggeration to state that the bricks were untouched by human hands from the time they left the brickyard until the bricklayers picked them up to set down in place in the mortar," boasted the writer of the construction notes. This feat was accomplished by using two brick hoppers, each with a capacity of about 20,000 bricks, with openings leading from the main floor. Trucks dumped the bricks through the floor openings into the hoppers. Each hopper fed the bricks through a slot in dump cars, each able to carry about 400 bricks. Workers hand-pushed these loaded cars along the industrial railway, then swung them on turntables to the material hoists. More workers helped raise the flat carts to the proper floor, pushed them off the hoist, and sent them along the railway tracks to the waiting bricklayer.

Because the production schedule required the raising of about 100,000 bricks every eight hours, two material hoists and 18 men were dedicated to the task. It was calculated that the salaries of 38 men were saved by keeping the bricks moving and having them in place at least three floors above the floor where the bricklayers were setting stone.

### Wiring the World's Tallest Building

"Suppose you were to wire a whole town at one time, for lights, power, telephones," wrote William McCrom, the man in charge of installing the electrical work in the Empire State. "Not only that—suppose the town wasn't there when you started, but was being built up as you worked. This will give you an idea of what it means to wire the tallest building man has yet put up."

But that was where the similarities ended, because how many of us need two-ton transformers one-quarter of a mile in

NO. 237    TAKEN 7/14/30
EMPIRE STATE BUILDING
WEST SIDE 5TH AVE., 33RD TO 34TH ST
NEW YORK, N.Y.
VIEW FROM
SHREVE, LAMB & HARMON, ARCHITE
STARRETT BROTHERS & EKEN INC.

the air (and put there by railway cars and chain blocks) with enough capacity to light 156,000 fifty-watt lamps as well as run the telephone system?

Because 1930s building codes required masonry fireproofing, a stone concrete fireproofing was poured around the sub-basement columns and the exterior basement columns. In addition, brick piers fireproofed the window mullions to prevent interior fires from damaging the walls. Finally, from the second basement to the 86th-floor roof, the large diagonal wind braces required the covering of an area of 91,000 square feet with wire mesh and cement fireproofing.

To save time and money, the concrete was mixed on site. Thus, two mixing plants were required; these were erected in the second basement. Material was fed into the plants from two bins in the first basement. Twelve yards of sand, 30 yards of cinder or crushed stone, and bagged cement from trucks on the main floor were dumped in and mixed. Operators continually opened the bags and fed cement to the two mixer plants.

Reinforcing materials such as wire mesh were raised on material hoists and form lumber was hoisted by steel derricks to the top from the street. They were then lowered through the steel frames and placed on the required floors. After the concrete hardened and gained enough strength to hold its own weight, workers removed the wood forms from below.

### Chrome-Nickel Steel—300 Tons of It

The time needed to install the exterior metal trim and spandrels was cut by 35 days. According to the construction notes, over 300 tons of chrome-nickel steel were used on the exterior of the building for window trim, mullions (vertical window dividers), and ornamental window heads. In addition, almost 300 tons of cast aluminum spandrels were used, more than on any other building of the time. This alloy is rust-resistant in a moist atmosphere, even in salt air—an important characteristic, considering Empire State's proximity to New York's harbor and the open sea.

### Limestone—200,000 Square Feet of It in Record Time

The 85 stories were completely enclosed on November 13, 1930, a gain of 17 days over the scheduled completion date of December 1. William Starrett wrote, "The exterior, except for a relatively small amount of granite used at the base and surrounding the main entrances, is of Indiana Limestone, about 200 thousand cubic feet of which was used, and to facilitate rapid construction, five stone cutting plants were used." Standardized sizes, together with a unique system of handling the stone from within the building, permitted rapid progress in building the exterior walls.

Like brick, limestone was kept ready three floors ahead of the floor where stone setters were working. The stone was unloaded from trucks inside the building and raised by the

*For thirteen months, workers busied themselves carving out a place in history for themselves and a place in the New York skyline for the Empire State Building.*

*Despite huge construction jobs in New York during the 1920s and '30s, like the Chrysler Building viewed in the background, Rockefeller Center, and the Empire State Building, there was an overall decline in construction jobs by nearly 24 percent. This worker seems to be contemplating his good fortune at finding employment, straddling a girder atop the Empire State.*

Construction workers endured many risks while they secured the iron and steel framework on the Empire State Building.

*How long would the Empire State Building endure as the highest building ever created by man, New Yorkers wondered in 1931. Was this the pinnacle of practicality?*

overhead monorail trolley to platform cars, which were pushed onto material hoists and placed on the upper floors using the railway system. All the stone cutting was completed at the local on-site plants; consequently, it was believed that a time record for erection of stonework was established at the Empire State Building.

Throughout the building, circuit wire and feeder cable was color-coded to push the job along. Cable was delivered in proper cutting lengths and tagged so that it could be put on the proper floor ahead of the pulling crew.

## Subcontractors' Materials

Not only did the comings and goings of regular materials handling and distribution have to be overseen but also each subcontractor on the job had to receive and move his own materials on schedule as well. The plasterer and floor fill-and-finish subcontractors had material hoists assigned to their exclusive use. Each subcontractor had to report to the foreman in charge of the main floor the hoist required, the day and number of hours it would be in use for raising his materials, not less than two days in advance. Drivers without prior authorization were not allowed to drive into the building.

**Subcontractors' materials included:**

Roofing and sheet metal—1,500 rolls of tar paper, 900 barrels of pitch

Exterior metal spandrels and trim—over 300 tons

Metal windows—600 tons of steel used in the manufacture, 12,000 pounds of bronze for hardware

Lathing and plastering materials—10,000 tons of plaster

Floor fill and finish

Finished carpentry and millwork

Metal doors and trim—1,900 doors

Elevator enclosures

Glass

Hardware

Miscellaneous iron

Aluminum

Mail chute construction materials—for 396 openings for the deposit of mail

Interior marble—328,096 square feet, or 2,297 tons, not including 15,000 bags of marble chips

Tile—about 105,00 square feet of various colors and sizes

Terrazzo materials

Vitreous glass partitions for toilets

Painting and decorating materials and supplies

Elevator supplies

Plumbing materials and equipment—51 miles of plumbing pipe

Heating and ventilating materials and equipment—54 miles

Electrical materials and equipment

Electrical fixtures

Refrigeration equipment

Vacuum cleaning system materials

Steel shutters and doors

Toilet accessories

Cork insulation and soundproofing materials

Damp-proofing materials—1,096 barrels of trowel mastic

Caulking materials—35 tons of caulking compound

Hydrozone equipment and supplies

*The Empire State's building lot, about two acres in size, was at least twice the size of most neighboring buildings and therefore had the ability to climb higher into the sky.*

*Craftsmen were the largest integral part of the huge team responsible for the accomplishment of the Empire State Building.*

## Fire Alarms

A fire alarm box had to be installed on every floor from the second basement to the 5th floor and on every alternate floor from the 6th to the 85th floors. At least once each night, a special key was inserted into each fire alarm box, which registered in the central office of the National District Telegraph Company, which immediately relayed a message to Fire Department Headquarters indicating that the circuit was in working order.

## Night Watchmen

A watchmen's tour system was developed to determine that all was well at the construction site. One watchman took care of every five floors and made half-hourly tours from 5:00 P.M. to 5:00 A.M. With a key he carried, the watchman had to punch each of the nine stations installed on the various floors; the stations were automatically registered in the central office of the National District Telegraph Company. This had to be done in proper sequence, and then the watchman returned to his transmitter box, where he signaled again to the central office that he had finished his tour. If all the stations were not punched in proper sequence, the key would not operate the transmitter station.

Each watchman was equipped with a small portable fire extinguisher and was familiar with the water supply system on each floor. This diligence was especially important on the floors where the riveters' forges were located.

If the signals were not received from the man on duty at the proper times, a telephone call was made to the head night watchman, who was dispatched to investigate.

In addition, phone calls were made every hour from each watchman to the head night watchman. This tour system was in operation every night and on Saturdays, Sundays, and holidays.

## Temporary Risers, Waste Lines, and Privies

A three- or four-inch riser was installed on every floor and equipped with two ¾-inch valve connections to which a fire hose could be attached in case of emergency. A full-sized watertight barrel was also placed on every floor to take care of overflow.

In addition, 4,000-gallon cypress water tanks were kept on the 21st, 42nd, 63rd, and 85th floors throughout the construction period. A pumping system with eight pumps was located in the basement for use with a temporary water supply.

To handle fire emergencies, a pump man and a hoisting engineer were on hand to lift firemen to the floor where they were needed. Firemen from various fire headquarters made daily inspections so that each company was thoroughly familiar with the construction of the building.

Temporary toilets made of cast iron were placed on every fourth floor for the workmen's use.

In this fashion, utilizing time, space, innovation, chutzpah—and, often, just plain common sense—the building that has always belonged to the people of the city of New York and to the people of America was also constructed by them.

*Ungarnished, the Empire State project would
reach higher than the Chrysler, but by a few feet
only. The mooring mast addition would add
another 200 feet and make the top of the
building a unique airport in the sky.*

NO. 361    TAKEN 12/3/30
EMPIRE STATE BUILDING
WEST SIDE 5TH AVE., 33RD TO 34TH STS.
NEW YORK, N. Y.

SHREVE, LAMB & HARMON, ARCHITECTS

*Buses and cars going up and down the avenues below probably looked like bugs, while people on the sidewalks, ever mindful of the fascinating view above their heads, most probably looked like swarming ants to the workers up high.*

Eighty percent of the steel was in place by August 1, when the building had reached to about the 50th story. During July, 20 stories of steel were placed in 24 regular working days.

By November 13, 1930, just eight months after the first steel was erected for Empire State, 85 stories were completed, 13 days ahead of schedule.

The complete building weighed 365,000 tons with a volume of about 37 million cubic feet. Of the 210 column footings supporting the structure, some of those in the tower section carried as much as 5,000 tons per column. About three million square feet of arches were set, requiring 62,000 cubic yards of anthracite cinder concrete and nearly three million feet of reinforcing mesh.

All this was accomplished "with only a negligible amount of overtime that is always incident to skyscraper construction, even when speed is not required," Starrett later wrote.[7] Finally, on a chilly November 13, 1930, masonry was completed. President Herbert Hoover, who pressed a button in Washington, D.C., to turn on the building's lights, made the official opening on May 1, 1931, a national event.

"Empire State seemed almost to float, like an enchanted fairy tower over New York. An edifice so lofty, so serene, so marvelously simple, so luminously beautiful, had never before been imagined…it will gleam in all its pristine beauty for our children's children to wonder at."[8]

**August 30, 1929**
Al Smith, president of Empire State, Inc., publishes plans for the greatest office building in the world.
**October 1, 1929**
Demolition of the Waldorf-Astoria Hotel begins.
**March 12, 1930**
Demolition of the Waldorf-Astoria Hotel is completed.
**March 17, 1930**
First steel for Empire State foundation is placed.
**June 5, 1930**
Exterior masonry is started.
**September 15, 1930**
Last steel is set on the 86th floor.
**September 19, 1930**
Al Smith lays the building's requisite cornerstone.
**November 13, 1930**
Masonry is completed.
**May 1, 1931**
Empire State is formally opened to the public, one month ahead of schedule.

*...a good deal of strolling on the thin edge of nothingness.*

Lewis W. Hine

# Chapter 4:
*Seven Million Man-Hours*

*I worked straight through five days and four nights [on the Parcel Post Building]. I was with the hoisting gang. The only time we got off was two hours for breakfast, one hour for lunch, one hour for supper, and one hour at night... I felt kind of ashamed of myself that I couldn't take it, falling asleep and all that...*

Chris Thorsten

The most astounding feature of the Empire State Building, one that today still stops people in their tracks, is the rapidity with which it was planned and constructed.

Within just 20 months of the architects' signing the first contracts in September 1929, and despite some 17 changes made during planning and construction, the Empire State was designed, engineered, erected, and ready for occupancy.

The fully enclosed building, 102 stories high, was built in 13 months.[1]

Credited with the military genius to pull off such a feat was Colonel William A. Starrett of Starrett Brothers, the construction company that won the bid to build what some called a "lonely dinosaur in the sky." [2]

Building a skyscraper, said Starrett, was the "peacetime equivalent of war." His methodical plans, devised in the Empire State Corporation's war rooms, allowed the Empire State Building to be completed in record time.

Steel girders still warm to the touch, having been milled in Pennsylvania only 15 to 20 hours earlier, were riveted into place by an endless supply of willing workers who knew that 10 other guys were ready to take their jobs. Total construction time was calculated at seven million man-hours spent during a period of one year and 45 days of work, including Sundays and holidays. The workforce consisted of some 3,400 people at any one time during peak periods. For the most skilled workers, pay was $1.92 per hour, with half an hour for lunch. Because the payroll was about $250,000 per week, workers were paid on site by an armored guard service.

If Chris Thorsten, a New York City ironworker, was accurate, fast-moving construction projects and little time off for the workers was de rigueur.

*I remember one job, it was the Parcel Post Building. Forty-third and Lexington Avenue. I worked straight through five days and four nights. I was with the hoisting gang. The only time we got off was two hours for breakfast, one hour for lunch, one hour for supper, and one hour at night... I felt kind of ashamed of myself that I couldn't take it, falling asleep and all that... That was a good job. We made money in those days.[3]*

The job could be dangerous, as Thorsten told a Works Progress Administration (WPA) interviewer in 1938:

*You ain't an ironworker unless you get killed... men hurt on all jobs. Take the Washington Bridge, the Triboro Bridge. Plenty of men hurt on those jobs. Two men killed on the Hotel New Yorker. I drove rivets all the way on that job. When I got hurt I was squeezed between a crane, and a collarbone broke and all the ribs in my body, and three vertebrae. I was laid up for four years.[4]*

According to "Notes on the Construction of the Empire State Building," published in the New York Skyscraper Museum's book *Building the Empire State*,[5] a total of six men were

*Workers securing rivets to hold the massive steel frame of the Empire State Building worked in teams of two, three, and four people to accomplish their task.*

reported killed while working on the construction of the Empire State Building: Giuseppe Tedesci, a laborer, died on January 31, 1930, as did L. DeMoninichi, also a laborer. Four months later it was the turn of ironworker Reuben Brown. Three people died in July, two of whom were carpenters: Sigus Andreasen and Frank Sullivan. The third victim was a pedestrian called Elizabeth Eagher. While crossing 34th Street west of Fifth Avenue, she was struck on the ankle by a piece of broken ironworker's plank. Blood poisoning, along with a complication arising from her injury, resulted in her death. And finally, on December 9, 1930, A. Carlson, a third carpenter, died.

"They are numbered among the unsung heroes of peace," the writer of the Empire State Building construction notes declared.

Despite this toll of human life, "what was impressive about the Empire State," says Donald Friedman in *Building the Empire State*, "was the builders' organization of the work, by which men and materials were present when and where they were needed." [6]

The first task, demolishing the four buildings—the Waldorf Hotel section, the Waldorf Annex, the Astoria section, and the Astor Court building—that constituted the Waldorf-Astoria Hotel that occupied the site, had to be completed efficiently and quickly so that materials could be transported to the building site. Any skywalker will tell you that tearing down a steel building is even more dangerous than building one. The demolition must be done by hand; if achieved too rapidly or with too much force, destabilization can result in a disordered and reckless collapse.

The construction notes said that actual demolition work on the group of buildings started on September 24, 1929, and that all the masonry and steel was completely demolished to the sidewalk level on February 3, 1930. The material disposed of from buildings down to sidewalk level comprised 16,508 loads of debris, each load with a capacity of 5.5 cubic yards—a total of 90,794 cubic yards. The steel down to sidewalk level weighed 12,097 tons.

The notes contain a summary of loads of material removed from the wrecked Waldorf-Astoria building, giving some sense of the enormity of this phase of the project. In total, 24,321 loads of material were taken from the old buildings.

Next came cellar and trench excavation, pier hold excavation, and pouring concrete footings for the massive steel columns at the base for the Empire State Building. Some 9,000 cubic yards of earth and over 17,000 cubic yards of rock were excavated. This work was carried on concurrently with the wrecking of the old walls and foundations.

Pier hole excavation involved 463 cubic yards of earth and 4,992 cubic yards of rock. The rock in many of the pier holes in the tower section was soft; in some cases the workers had to dig 30 to 40 feet below sub-basement floor elevation to strike the hard rock necessary to pass the test required before concrete could be poured. Finally, nearly 4,000 cubic yards of concrete were poured into 210 piers.

*The heater placed about 10 rivets into a hot forge and then used tongs to pull out the red hot rivets and toss them in the air to his teammate.*

Anyone, whether a construction worker, an administrator, or a bookkeeper, can appreciate the level of expertise needed to complete what was then the world's tallest and largest building, which had to be finished within one year.

## The Organization

Directly in charge of the work was the job superintendent, 38-year-old John W. Bowser, who needed not only a thorough knowledge of building construction but also "an aggressive personality, tempered with the qualities of tact." [7] Under the superintendent's direction were the following departments:

Job runners had the responsibility of "receiving, filing and distributing of all plans and shop drawings, interpreting of plans for job organization and subcontractors, preparation of contracts, change orders and estimating for tenant changes and variations from original plans, expediting material and mill and shop inspection."

The Construction Department was "in charge of all construction work, such as masonry, stone, concrete, carpentry and has direct supervision of all the work installed by subcontractors." Also included in this department were the civil and mechanical engineering departments, which conducted field inspections.

The Accounting Division included "auditing and bookkeeping, timekeeping and payroll departments, purchasing and receiving departments." It was also in charge of keeping track of losses or gains in original cost estimates.

The Payroll Division collected the number of hours each individual worked daily and posted it on the payroll, which ran, on average, at approximately $250,000 per week.

The Production Department took physical inventories of the materials on hand and checked those numbers against quantities surveyed in place in the field. The job superintendent used these figures along with the cost of labor to determine whether he was running above or below cost estimates.

"Perhaps the best way," the construction notes say, "to get a cross section of the varied activities of the many men employed on a building operation of this size is to glance at the job diary.... Our records show that Thursday, August 14, 1930, was the day upon which the greatest number of men [and perhaps women] were employed—namely 3,439 of whom 1,928 were working for the Builders and 1,511 for the various sub-contractors." [8]

The exhaustive list comprises Supervising Overhead personnel, including one superintendent, one assistant superintendent, one job runner, two assistant job runners, one accountant, one purchasing agent, one engineer, one assistant to the superintendent, four stenographers, one plan clerk, one telephone operator, and one office boy.

Operating Overhead personnel included one assistant superintendent, one civil engineer, seven assistant civil engineers, one mechanical inspector, one electrical inspector, one elevator inspector, one ornamental iron inspector, one

| Materials | Loads Removed from Wrecked Buildings above Sidewalks | Loads Removed from Old Walls and Foundations |
|---|---:|---:|
| Debris | 15,738 | 6,246 |
| Firewood | 770 | 56 |
| Structural steel and misc. | 1,184 | 298 |
| Scrap iron | | |
| Scrap copper | 26 | |
| Scrap brass | 3 | |
| Scrap lead | 1 | |
| Total | 17,722 | 6,559 |

*While some parts of the Waldorf-Astoria Hotel—like the flagpole, bricks, or a piece of iron rail fence—were considered mementos by some, the large bulk of its remains had to be disposed of rather unceremoniously.*

caulking inspector, one general inspector, two expediters, one timekeeper, one assistant timekeeper, two cost clerks, two clerks, one production clerk, two distribution clerks, 27 checkers, two storekeepers, 31 watchmen, one porter, and one engineer.

Further, the payroll consisted of two bricklayer foremen, their bricklayer deputies, 281 bricklayers, 10 bricklayer's apprentices, nine bricklayer labor pushers, 391 laborers, one general labor foreman, one arch labor foreman, 11 arch labor pushers, 334 arch laborers, one stone setter foreman, two stone setter deputies, 39 stone setters, four stonecutter deputies, and 32 stonecutters.

Add to that one derrickman foreman, five derrickman pushers, 123 derrickmen, 43 carpenter helpers, one excavator pusher, 44 excavators, one driller pusher, and 15 drillers—also, one cement finisher pusher, 49 cement finishers, one pipefitter foreman, three pipefitters, one elevator constructor pusher, five elevator constructors, and 12 elevator constructor's helpers.

Finally, one ironwork pusher, nine ironworkers, one master mechanic, 25 hoisting engineers, two assistant hoisting engineers, three plasterer laborers, three rock men, one burner, two maintenance men, and 20 water boys.

An additional 1,511 similar employees were brought to the job by such subcontractors as J. Livingston and Company (electricians for temporary light and power); J. L. Murphy, Inc. (plumbing); Baker, Smith and Company (heating and ventilating); Asbestos Construction Company (pipe covering); Martin Conroy and Sons (lathing and plastering); Traitel Marble Company (interior marble); and Jacob Ringle and Son (roofing and sheet metal work).

As was typical in the construction industry of the time, all hiring was done before 8:00 A.M. on the first floor of the timekeeper's shanty-office. Each man hired was given a hiring ticket with his name, class, rate of pay, and time and date hired. He presented this ticket at the timekeeper's office, where a personnel card was filled in and his record of earnings kept for income tax purposes. He was assigned a number and a small brass disk, which was given to him each morning when he reported to work and which he gave up at the end of each workday.

During the day, field time checkers visited every man on the building once in the morning and once in the afternoon and asked him to show his disk. On Friday, which was payday, he received an aluminum disk bearing his number; upon presenting it to the paymaster, he received his pay.

Lord's chain of restaurants was given the food concession for the building project. At the restaurant owner's expense, five lunch stands were constructed on the 3rd, 9th, 24th, 47th, and 64th floors. Many of the men brought their own lunches but often bought hot coffee, milk, or other beverages at the lunch stands.

## The Rocky Road

This phenomenal, highly organized team approach became a hallmark in the construction industry. It was preplanning and precision timing that allowed the construction of the Empire State to exceed even its developers' expectations. But not everything went as smooth as glass for Starrett Brothers and Eken. Rumors and news stories abounded with "malicious propaganda" that adequate protection of human life was disregarded in the feverish anxiety of the builders, owners, and architects to establish a record for speed in constructing the building. The purpose of these rumors seemed to be political. The author of the building construction notes accuses as "character assassins" those who even during the 1928 presidential campaign painted a picture of Al Smith as a man who would "sponsor such a condition" and then suppress the truth about it.

The note-writer defends the construction's safety record by indicating that the engineering firm had its own independent safety inspectors constantly on the job in addition to those of three agencies—the City of New York Building Department, the New York State Labor Department, and Employers Liability Assurance Company.

It was considered "extremely regrettable" that seven people lost their lives during the building of Empire State: six workers and one pedestrian. But, says the notes' author, this was simply due to the normal hazards of modern building construction and not to "indifference on the part of those in charge."

There was the prospect of labor trouble, too. On two projects in Newark and Cincinnati, ironworkers struck, closing construction for six weeks. The Empire State was not involved in the strike even though it did employ nonunion ironworkers.

Paul Starrett felt the strain of erecting the Empire State Building in such a short amount of time. He claimed the stress was too much for him and caused him to suffer a rather severe nervous breakdown.[9] However, many people who work in the construction field believe that most architects, engineers, and builders will never have Starrett's good fortune, which was to have worked on one of the finest buildings ever constructed. No one involved in Empire State was a lone genius. The unique collaborative effort to overcome problems, according to architect Donald Friedman, has never been surpassed.

*Rumors and news stories abounded with "malicious propaganda" that adequate protection of human life was disregarded in the feverish anxiety of the builders, owners, and architects to establish a record for speed in constructing the building. The purpose of these rumors seemed to be political.*

*Name a walk of life and you might have found someone working on the Empire State Building who had trudged down it toward this stellar accomplishment. Alas, many of the workers, now passed on, did not understand at the time the significance of what they were helping to build.*

*Stare up at such a building and it fairly dominates one's mind and body.*[1]

Frederick Simpich

# Chapter 5:
*Amazing Statistics and Empire State Building Trivia*

Despite opening at exactly the wrong time, at least in terms of the developers' original goal of making money by leasing office space and cornering the lucrative Manhattan real estate business, the Empire State Building became a celebrity as the world's tallest building and a common setting for spectacular dramas.

In the building's early days, unemployment was rampant and "rent" parties were de rigueur in some sectors. Attendees drank a little booze, played games, and threw in 25 cents so the tenants could hold off the landlord another month. The Empire State did not reach full occupancy for many years and began throwing its own rent parties, so to speak, by charging a fee[2] to visit the observatories. If not for the millions of paying visitors each year, Empire State might have been a losing financial proposition all around.

The building's tenants have been good, solid businesses, but not the blue-chip companies that would have given the address some pizzazz. The days have passed when the U.S. State Department regularly arranged visits for foreign heads of state who wanted to pose on the observation deck. Fidel Castro is said to have grinned from ear to ear when he visited!

Although it never became a prestigious business address, the Empire State Building occupies a special place in many people's hearts. It continues to be and perhaps always has been a building for the people—what they consider quintessential New York.

The Empire State continues to be one of the most culturally inspiring places on earth. On a typical day, 4,000 to 6,000 people are drawn to the observatory to marvel. Visitors from all over the world can readily recall its vistas, the building's instantly recognizable profile on the Manhattan skyline, and the evident pride Americans take in this very American building, represented in the pictures and words of countless stories, poems, television shows, and movies.

But promoters have often had to scramble to ensure Empire State's place in the sky.

## Cashing In on Height

When it looked like the newly constructed Chrysler Building was too close for comfort in terms of height, that tenacious pair of Empire State promoters, Al Smith and John Raskob, came up with a great idea for the top of their building. They decided that the structure's chapeau would be a mooring mast for the latest in transcontinental travel. Dirigibles would cross the Atlantic, then appear over Manhattan and glide to the Empire State Building to dock at the world's tallest building. Passengers would transfer from airship to skyscraper, and an elevator would whisk them to

street level. New Yorkers would be treated to the sight of the behemoth hovering overhead.

"The builder's lawyers even prepared a thick brief, arguing, amongst other things, that owners of neighboring buildings could not sustain a claim of trespass when they found dirigibles overhead," wrote Lester A. Reingold in the July 2000 *Air & Space Smithsonian*.[3]

Ungarnished, the Empire State project would reach higher than the Chrysler, but by a few feet only. The mooring mast addition would add another 200 feet and make the top of the building a unique airport in the sky.

Or was the mooring mast just "the looniest building scheme since the Tower of Babel?"[4]

By opening day, May 1, 1931, the bullet-shaped mooring mast, decorated with the requisite chrome-nickel steel and faceted glass, was ready. Winches for pulling in arriving dirigibles had been installed, along with a passenger lounge and customs and ticket offices. But while the building's framework could handle the 50-ton pull of a moored dirigible, no one had thought about the shifting air currents caused by air drafts from the height of Manhattan's skyscrapers. When one considers that atop the Empire State snow falls up instead of down, it is easy to recognize the type of updraft that the dirigibles would have had to fight against to land, or even to remain motionless for the time needed to allow passengers to disembark. Dirigibles also required several ropes for handling rather than the single rope that was originally intended. When combining these logistics, the sheer danger of the possibility of millions of cubic feet of hydrogen gas exploding over a densely populated city deemed the mooring unusable.

The idea was full of holes. Passengers might have a lounge, but making their way to the New York streets below was going to be a major hassle. The walkway was narrow, the door small, and stairways to the elevator were more like ladders.

Smith tried to wrangle a way for the Navy, who had begun exploring the use of dirigibles in the U.S. in the 1920s for scouting purposes, to get involved with the project, but to no avail. Germany's Zeppelin Company, whose monopoly on passenger airship service was uncontested, wasn't enthusiastic either, given the safety and maneuvering difficulties presented by Smith's idea. It became increasingly clear that bringing dirigibles into midtown Manhattan was not a good idea.

Other than a quick drop of a bundle of newspapers from a dirigible at the Empire State's mooring mast used as a public relations gimmick, Smith and Raskob gave up on the scheme of making the top of the building a human passenger landing station.

## A Mooring Mast by any Other Name…

The mooring mast that capped the Empire State Building, at first simply to creep past the Chrysler Building's pointed top, went through a true metamorphosis, starting out as a mooring mast for dirigibles and ending up a telecommunications tower.

Indeed, more than beautiful colored lights and music comes from the top of the Empire State Building. The mooring mast remained, and it became an asset in the early 1950s when it turned out to be a spectacular radio and television transmitter.

According to Lydia Ruth, Director of Public Relations for the Empire State Building, Empire State has always had broadcasting facilities on top; they were just improved upon and made taller, bigger, and stronger over the years. Radio broadcasts have been sent from the building since opening night. Beginning in late 1931, NBC began experimental transmissions from its TV station, which was also located on top of the building. By 1950, a permanent TV tower was erected, contracted to the American Bridge Company, a division of U.S. Steel, for design and installation.

Edward Buechele was the chief engineer in the drawing room at American Bridge's Shiffler plant in Pittsburgh in the 1950s. He also represented American Bridge during the installation of the mast.

"The top of the building was the tallest point in the city, and this has obvious advantages for low-frequency transmission, looking seaward, of course," said Bill Shafer, Buechele's grandson. Low frequencies need long (tall) antennae. The Empire State Building had an antenna in the early days of AM radio, but a larger mast was required as use increased.

Kathryn Buechele Schneider recalls when her father, Edward Buechele, would come home from working on the design of the Empire State broadcasting mast. He was such a perfectionist, she remembers, that he would drive her mother crazy talking about this right angle and that angle. And "dammit, they forgot to do thus and so and it has to be done all over again!" Buechele would exhaust himself with the details of the monumental task of building the broadcast tower for major television and radio stations, and immediately following his after-dinner coffee, he would go upstairs and take a nap. "I hated to listen to those dinner conversations," recalls Mrs. Schneider, who as a young girl wished he would pay more attention to her than to the radio tower.[5]

But for metropolitan New York, Buechele's perfectionism and extraordinary effort paid off. Completed at a cost of $3 million, the TV tower is still the world's most powerful and far-reaching. From Empire State's summit, all nine of greater New York's television stations transmit programs throughout five states. The tower is the property of the Empire State Building, although the antennae attached to it belong to the individual broadcasting stations.

Today, above the 86th-floor observation deck, Metro Networks monitors traffic conditions in the New York area by way of two broadcast cameras and microwave antennae on the east and west sides of the building. The traffic information is broadcast on New York City's major television and radio stations.

The tower, which can withstand wind pressure of 50 pounds per square inch, is equipped with three intercommunications systems that connect reception devices to antennae to transmitters and associated equipment housed on the building's upper floors. Lightning rod and aircraft warning lights are also attached to the antenna tower. Professional tower climbers are employed for necessary maintenance and regular relamping of obstruction lights.

The Empire State Building also houses transmission facilities for the communications operations of the New York Telephone Company. In addition, the building serves as the nerve center for network television remote relays and accommodates paging services, microwave operations, two-way radio facilities, and the Multipoint Distribution Service facility, which provides closed-circuit broadcasts of movies and sporting events to selected sites in New York City.

*The mooring mast tower can withstand wind pressure of 50 pounds per square inch and is now equipped with three intercommunications systems. Professional tower climbers are employed for maintenance and changing lights.*

## Bits and Pieces

A *New York Herald Tribune* writer claimed in 1952 that to most New Yorkers, "the top of the Empire State is as remote as Mars" and that many of the people who worked in the building had never been topside. Not even Mrs. Audrie Wilkie, a Yonkers native whose father, William Wall, was employed as an ironworker on Empire State's construction, had visited the crowning glory of her father's craft until she went many years after its completion—as a married woman! But, said Mrs. Wilkie at the Empire State Building's 70th anniversary celebration, "I miss him so much and I know he's looking down at me and being so proud that his little baby [Mrs. Wilkie was an infant when her father worked on the Empire State] is here tonight to celebrate the anniversary of the Empire State Building."

Whether you've already visited or not, and no matter where you grew up, you are surely familiar with the Empire State Building. It belongs to the world. Here are some amazing statistics of "our tallest sky-piercing pinnacle," whose 210 supporting columns bear a load "distributed so evenly that the weight on any given square inch was no greater than that normally borne by a French heel," according to associate architect R. H. Shreve.

Of course, the most talked-about statistic regarding the Empire State Building is the amount of time it took to complete the project. As the title of this book indicates, just 13 months elapsed between the beginning of construction and the building's grand opening on May 1, 1931. Other figures take into account additional aspects of the entire project, which included the demolition of the old Waldorf-Astoria Hotel to clear the site.

For example, 20 months passed between the signing of the contracts with the builders and architects in September 1929 and the grand opening. General excavation began on January 22, 1930, 15 months before the opening. The excavation was finished and actual building commenced on March 17, 1930, bringing construction time to 13 months.

Here are some of the many interesting tidbits of information about the Empire State Building, a structure that via the arts, media, and tourism is familiar to one and all:

- 1,472 feet (448 meters) in height to the top of the antennae
- 1,250 feet (391 meters) to the 102nd-floor observatory
- 1,050 feet (320 meters) to the 86th-floor observatory
- 210 steel columns in vertical frame, 12 of these running the entire height of the building (excluding the mooring mast)
- Volume: 37 million cubic feet
- Area of site: 83,860 square feet
- Cost, including land: $40,948,900
- Cost of building alone: $24,718,000 (the expected cost of $50 million did not materialize due to the Great Depression)
- 102 floors—it was the tallest building in the world when it was completed, surpassing the Chrysler Building
- Some seven million man-hours of labor in its construction
- 3,439 workers were employed on Thursday, August 14, 1930—the day with the greatest number of workers
- 3.7 million visitors per year
- Snow falling down is an event at the top of the Empire State, where snow usually falls up due to upsweeping winds.

*When it was built, the shadow of the Empire State Building stretched across the East River and into Brooklyn.*

**Here is some less familiar or typical information:**

- In 1941, when Pearl Harbor was attacked, bringing the United States into World War II, the top of the Empire State Building was used for antiaircraft surveillance. Stairwells and fire stairs in the middle of the building became air raid shelters. All windows and the tower were blacked out.

- If all the materials used to build the Empire State had been delivered at once, a train 57 miles long would have been needed. You'd find the locomotive standing in New York while the caboose was still in Bridgeport, Connecticut.

- One workman working every day would have had to work 25 years to mortar the 10 million bricks in the Empire State.

- The Empire State's 200,000 cubic feet of stone would have required a train of more than 400 flatcars.

- There are 1,172 miles of elevator cable rubber-covered wire, enough to reach from New York to Jacksonville, Florida.

- Under the floors and in the walls of the Empire State Building run 75 miles of main water pipes. For heating, 50 miles of radiator pipes run throughout the building.

- The Empire State's outer walls contain 730 tons of aluminum and stainless steel, the lightest metals available.

- The Empire State sported 6,000 pairs of office telephone cables for 3,000 trunk line switchboards and 5,000 station telephones.

- The Empire State claimed 400 fire hose connections and a completely self-contained fire department.

- For power and lights, two million feet of electrical wires run through the Empire State, equal to 380 miles, the distance between New York and Buffalo. The Empire State, in 1931, used as much electricity as a city the size of Albany.

- The building's steel frame, 60,000 tons in weight, was long enough to have been rolled into a double railroad track between New York and Saratoga Springs.

- The Empire State contains sockets for 350,000 lightbulbs.

- The building's 63 self-leveling elevators have 1,232 doors.

- There is enough floor space to shelter 80,000 people.

- It takes one man a full day's work just replacing burned out lightbulbs in the tower alone.

- The building needs 250 cleaners to keep it in shape.

- Temperatures at the top of Empire State range from 3° to 9°F (16° to 12°C) lower than at the street. The record difference in temperatures is −16°F (−26°C) at the top of the Empire State and 8°F (−13°C) down on Fifth Avenue.

- More than 200 species of insects have been sucked up by strong winds and collected on the Empire State Building.

- In September 1948, on a particularly dark and gusty night, over 500 migrating birds including common yellowthroats, American redstarts, and ovenbirds, were found dead and scores injured after flying at a lower than usual altitude, having crashed into the Empire State Building. For this reason, the top of the building is occasionally left dark on foggy or rainy nights in the spring and fall to protect migratory birds in bad weather that "might otherwise be attracted to the floodlights that illuminate the 72nd to 102nd floors and rush toward them like months to a flame."

- It once rained red at the top of the building—red clay particles from outside the city had been sucked up.

- A white rainfall turned out to be a "barley blizzard" from a nearby brewery.

- Does the building sway or bend in the wind? Minneapolis Honeywell installed a gyroscope on the building and found that in a high wind the Empire State shifts no more than ¼ inch off center, with a total sway of ½ inch.

- You can see snakes on the top of the Empire State—without imbibing mind-altering substances. Certain atmospheric conditions create a strong wind that splits around the building and produces a mirage that looks like an undulating python.

- You can get an electric thrill on top of the Empire State if you are wearing rubber-soled shoes. Shuffle your feet and kiss your sweetie on a dry day—and wow!

- The tower had been struck by lightning 500 times by the 1950s—19 times in one storm. The tower acts like a lightning rod, which shields other buildings in a ¼-mile radius.

- You can experience St. Elmo's fire, a type of continuous electric spark called a glow discharge, on top of the Empire State. You've seen it many times before, inside fluorescent tubes. If you stand on the observation tower on a night when an electrical storm is brewing and reach over the parapet, you may be able to pick a handful of cold blue flame out of the air. During the day when you can't see the visual effect, you can still hear a sound like a thousand eggs frying.

In 1932, the Polish Olympic ski team tried to launch a new sport by racing to the top of the Empire State in 21 minutes. The Poles held the record until 1978, when the New York Road Runners Club revived the sport. The course is up 86 flights of stairs, totaling 1,576 steps.

**But wait—there's more:**

• In 1932, the Polish Olympic ski team tried to launch a new sport by racing to the top of the Empire State in 21 minutes. On the 102nd floor, they ran into the Czech team that had just beaten them in Lake Placid. The Czechs challenged the Poles to a race, but apparently the building's management stepped in. The Poles held the record until 1978, when the New York Road Runners Club revived the sport. The course is up 86 flights of stairs, totaling 1,576 steps. In 2001, Paul Crake of Australia made the run in 9 minutes, 37 seconds.

• In 1947, Empire State, Inc., installed huge carillon bells to pump out Christmas carols to shoppers below. However, no one could hear them except over in Coney Island, some 16 miles away. The bells were removed after that.

• And where were you at 5:27 P.M. on November 9, 1965, the moment the Great Northeast Blackout began? The failure of a relay device in Ontario, Canada, threw 80,000 square miles of America's east coast into darkness. Because it was rush hour, some 30 million people were involved, including some 800,000 who were trapped in trains above and belowground. In Manhattan, St. Patrick's Cathedral became one of many refuges for the stranded. The Empire State was the worst hit among office buildings; 13 elevators holding 96 people were stuck in midair. The tightly packed passengers had to stay put until a hole was smashed in the wall of the lift shaft at about 10:45 that night. Some of those with a sense of humor organized a Blackout Club to while away the time…no cigar smoking allowed.

• In 1962, the building got its first bath. Thirty men took six months to scrub down 500,000 square feet of limestone. The job cost $200,000. Three thousand gallons of waterproof coating were rubbed into the limestone surface at that time.

• In the early 1970s, the skyscraper race suddenly sprang to life again, and the North Tower of the World Trade Center was built, reaching 1,350 feet. Robert Jones of Shreve, Lamb, and Harmon suggested adding 11 floors to Empire State. The idea was to raze the building at about the 81st floor and add a new 33-story structure on top, making Empire State 1,494 feet tall and the world's tallest building once again. But the plan never developed in detail. Indeed, the building's fame does not rest on height alone.

• In 1992, the lights of the Empire State Building were turned out, perhaps for one of the only times since World War II, by its owner, Harry Helmsley, the so-called king of Manhattan real estate, when his wife, Leona, was put in prison for tax evasion. Helmsley turned them back on the next day.

• In 1992, the building's 6,300 window frames were replaced with the current red frames.

• On Sunday, October 25, 1998, two daredevils parachuted off the Empire State Building in pink parachutes, floated to West Thirty-fourth Street below, and disappeared. They had apparently jumped from the observation deck on the 86th floor.

• Did you know you could get married on the top of the Empire State Building? Each year, 14 couples from all over the world are selected from the many who write to say why they would like to be married at one of the most famous buildings in the world.

The Empire State has witnessed many good times, trysts, weddings—and a good deal of drama caused by accidents, explosions, arsonists, and those tired of living. But the building continues to give to the people of New York, the people of America, and to the world. "Such was the task undertaken that wintry day, early in 1930, when the deep concrete foundations were completed and the actual construction of Empire State began."

Is it any wonder that the Empire State Building is known as the Eighth Wonder of the World? Surely many things, including King Kong, are touted as "eighth wonders," but the Empire State Building says it in art. In the Thirty-fourth Street lobby is a series of paintings by Roy Sparkia and Renee Nemerov showing the building comfortably—and rightfully—next to the seven wonders of the ancient world. According to a study by the National Park Service, the Empire State Building remains one of the top 10 destinations for U.S. travelers, receiving in excess of 4.3 million visitors from every state in the U.S. and almost every country in the world each year.

## Empire State in the Movies

"A building with this much character can't seem to keep itself out of the movies," says the official web site, and the Empire State Building has been the site or backdrop for some 120—including, of course, *King Kong* (1933).

RKO Studios' Production 601, otherwise known as *King Kong*, was inspired by the jungle expeditions of its director and producer, Ernest B. Schoedsack and Merian C. Cooper. The low-budget film, never even nominated for an Academy Award, rescued the studio from near bankruptcy and allowed it to continue production until 1953. *King Kong* is said to be one of the all-too-rare monster movies that does not fall into the science-fiction category.

The fairy tale story of beauty killing the beast was reworked to become this classic movie, which despite certain technical flaws (including a "native" falling off the high wall and knocking over a prop) remains as exciting today as it was when first released at Radio City Music Hall in New York. The success of the film lies in its representation of nonconformity battling social convention, a rebellion born out of the Great Depression. Ultimately, and tragically, even Kong fails and is subjugated by conformity.

The film was made over three years at a cost of $420,000, most of which was used to build a 50-foot-high model of Kong. The ape's face measured seven feet from hairline to chin, while actor Carmen Nigro, dressed in a monkey suit, was used for the long shots. Animation was performed with 18-inch models.

Cooper had first put forward the title *Kong*, but it was rejected because it sounded too much like the title of his previous film, *Chang*, and Schoedsack's *Rango*. The film was originally publicized as *The Beast*. In January 1931, the film was advertised as *Kong*, but Schoedsack's wife, Ruth Rose, who wrote the final version of the film, called it *The Eighth Wonder of the World*. In February 1933, it finally became *King Kong*. Schoedsack and Cooper appear in the film as the flight commander and chief observer in the airplane that shoots Kong down from the Empire State Building.

More *King Kong* trivia: The large gates used on Kong's island were left over from the set for the film *King of Kings*. The same gates appeared again in *Gone with the Wind*, where they were destroyed along with other old sets in the scene in which Atlanta burns.

Besides *King Kong* and a host of films from the 1930s, '40s, '50s, and '60s, other movies that have utilized the Empire State Building include *Taxi Driver* (1976), directed by Martin Scorcese, a rather dark film about a psychotic Vietnam War veteran played by Robert De Niro; director Rob Reiner's romantic comedy *When Harry Met Sally* (1989), starring Billy Crystal and Meg Ryan, and these perpetual favorites:

### An Affair to Remember (1957)

Called by some a scene-for-scene remake of the 1939 film *Love Affair*, by the same director, Leo McCarey, *An Affair to Remember* is said to be equally as enjoyable when Cary Grant and Deborah Kerr, both engaged to be married to other people, meet and fall in love during an ocean voyage. The lovers agree that if they still feel the same about one another at the end of six months, they will meet again at the top of the Empire State Building.

### Sleepless in Seattle (1993)

Eight-year old Jonah Baldwin is caught between his own unhappiness, missing his mother who died from cancer 18 months ago, and feeling the sadness and loneliness of his father, Sam. On a particularly melancholy Christmas Eve, Jonah calls a radio talk-show psychologist and asks for help. Forced onto the phone by his son, Sam reluctantly opens up and talks about his dead wife. Across the country in Baltimore, Annie Reed is listening to the same syndicated show. Engaged to another man, she begins to daydream, however, about meeting Sam. Meet him she does, thanks to young Jonah, at the top of the Empire State Building—on Valentine's Day no less. Clips from *An Affair to Remember* are used throughout, reminding us perhaps of the endurance of love and the permanence of the Empire State Building as a place where love often blooms.

But the Empire State Building has been celebrated in song, poetry, and prose as well. David Wiesner's *Sector 7* is about a little boy visiting the Empire State Building. He visits this flying machine that makes clouds. Joe Neumann's *Joe and the Skyscraper* is about the building of the Empire State as seen through the eyes of a 16-year-old. Roald Dahl's *James and the Giant Peach* is about a young boy's fanciful arrival in New York and at the Empire State Building.

*1993 film* Sleepless in Seattle. *This is probably the most memorable scene, where Tom Hanks and Meg Ryan are reunited at the top of the Empire State Building.*

*Clips from* An Affair to Remember *are used throughout* Sleepless in Seattle, *reminding us perhaps of the endurance of love and the permanence of the Empire State Building as a place where love often blossoms.*

*The fairy tale* Beauty and the Beast *was reworked to become the all-time classic movie,* King Kong. *King Kong climbed Empire State instead of the Chrysler Building, which had been the film director's first choice, but Chrysler's seductive curves proved too slippery for Kong to scale safely.*

**COMPLETE NEWS**
PLUS
**PICTURE MAGAZINE**
PLUS
**COLOR COMICS**
**5¢**

**Week-End Edition**

# New York Post 7

FOUNDED 1801, VOLUME 144, NO. 212. COPYRIGHT, 1945, NEW YORK POST CORPORATION.

NEW YORK, SATURDAY, JULY 28, 1945

# EXTRA

# BOMBER HITS EMPIRE STATE BLG.

## Good Luck, Bad Luck—Who Knows?

*I didn't see the B-25 ram into the ESB that Saturday morning, but I did see it embedded in the…on the…34th Street side. I used to go to the bank every morning with an escort for change and so forth and this bomber had hit and penetrated this Saturday morning. It was too early for the department stores to open. It was heavily overcast and they weren't high enough, or they were lackadaisical…I don't know…there were all kinds of stories floating around…and I used to go to that bank…it was the Chemical National Bank of the ESB for our change and we had a bank account there and so forth…but that Saturday morning when we heard about it and I looked up because I worked diagonally across the street on 35th Street and 5th Avenue we couldn't see the bomber, until the fog dissipated a couple of days later, or a day later. Then we could see this monster sticking out…the fuselage and tail…right in there…well needless to say they took it out and patched it and you'd never know…but because it was a Saturday morning two of the engines went right through onto the 33rd Street side and fell down 72 stories. Knocked down nine or 11 elevators and killed 22 people who were in the offices early…flames and gasoline and all. Over 20,000 people worked there every day, but being Saturday, there were just a few people in there that early in the morning…so that's the Empire State Building.* [6]

On July 28, 1945, a B-25 bomber, lost in fog, rammed into the Empire State Building. Few now remember the event, and even fewer know of the miraculous survival of the woman who fell 75 stories when the cables to her elevator were severed in that accident.

Lieutenant Colonel William F. Smith, Jr., a decorated veteran of 100 combat missions, was piloting the bomber from his home base in Bedford, Massachusetts, to Newark, New Jersey. But a thick fog covering the city forced air traffic controllers to tell Smith to land at LaGuardia Airport in New York. Smith, however, apparently believing he could maneuver safely through the fog, asked and received permission to fly on to Newark, on the other side of Manhattan from LaGuardia. The last thing the air traffic controller told Smith was, "At the present time, I can't see the top of the Empire State Building."

Some say in retrospect that Smith should never have been cleared to proceed to Newark. Disoriented by the dense fog, he apparently believed he was on Manhattan's west side. Instead, he suddenly found himself passing the Chrysler Building. To miss it, he "went right rudder" and, at 200 miles per hour, careened on a path down Forty-second Street and banked south over Fifth Avenue toward the Empire State. He tried to pull up, but it was too late. At 9:40 that Saturday morning, the B-25 slammed into the 79th floor of the Empire State Building.

Luckily, the accident occurred on a weekend, and only about 1,500 people were in the building compared with the 10,000 to 15,000 on an average weekday. Still, 14 died in the accident—11 in the building, plus Colonel Smith and two of his passengers. Receiving the brunt of the collision was the Catholic War Relief Office on the 79th floor, directly in the path of the bomber. Eight relief office workers were killed.

But there was more trauma to come—and a bit of good luck in the end.

William Roberts of *Elevator World* wrote, "Unaware that the plane's other engine and part of its landing gear had fallen through the elevator shaft, rescue workers used elevators to transport casualties."

Unbeknownst to rescuers, when the hoist and governor cables of one of the elevators had been severed, ropes to other cars had been weakened. Despite all this, the elevators had to be used to transport those severely injured, including Betty Lou Oliver, an elevator operator. As the plane hit, Oliver was blown out of her post on the 80th floor and badly burned. After receiving first aid on the site, she was put in another car to go down to an ambulance. As the elevator doors closed, rescue workers heard what sounded like a gunshot but what was, in fact, the snapping of elevator cables weakened by the crash. The car with Oliver inside, now at the 75th floor, plunged to the sub-basement, a fall of over 1,000 feet. Rescuers had to cut a hole in the car to get to the badly injured elevator operator.

Despite the awful knowledge of her narrow escape, Oliver survived, due in large part to the elevator safety devices that served their function, though perhaps not as envisioned. The elevator car safety could not set because the governor cable had been severed by the plane's impact. Therefore, other factors contributed to slowing the elevator and "cushioning" its fall. As the elevator fell, the compensating cables, hanging from beneath the car, piled up in the pit and acted as a coiled spring, slowing the elevator. [7]

Unlike the tragic events following the collision of two commercial jetliners into the World Trade Center towers on September 11, 2001, the integrity of the Empire State Building was not affected. The cost of the damage done by the 1945 crash was $1 million and death and injury was kept to a minimum, while the 2001 attacks caused untold millions of dollars in damage and the loss of thousands of lives. The World Trade Center's collapse following the jet collisions has been attributed to the intense heat temperatures of the fires caused by two fully fuel-loaded commercial airplanes, which affected the integrity of the towers' steel skeletons.

*In 1945, an Army Air Corps B-25 twin-engine bomber plane crashed into the 79th floor of the building in dense fog.*

## Is New York a Safe Haven for Its Signature Building?

Since the terrorist attacks on the World Trade Center the available office space in the Empire State Building has tripled to 300,000 square feet, or about 15 percent of the building. Reports indicate that an increasing number of tenants are leaving the building, once again the tallest in New York, fearing another terrorist attack. "There's a feeling the second shoe is going to drop," one real estate broker was reported as saying. "Tenants really fear something else will happen and they will be next." [8]

A 110-meter mast atop the World Trade Center was a broadcast hub for the entire New York City area, supporting FM radio as well as nine TV stations, including local affiliates of CBS, NBC, and ABC, according to a special report by Samuel Moore of IEEE Spectrum online.[9] When the tower was hit on September 11, transmission from the mast was among the casualties.

In the aftermath of the attack, WCBS activated a 35-year-old backup transmitter located atop the Empire State Building and subsequently also installed a new 30-kilowatt transmitter, originally intended for the World Trade Center. Two other stations also relocated to the Empire State Building following the WTC attacks.

The Empire State Building is already crowded with transmitters and antennae. Stations like WWOR and WNYW have had to install temporary antennae below the building's antenna mast. The building shares the World Trade Center's fame as a U.S. landmark and was evaluated in response to bomb threats since the September 11 attacks on more than one occasion. The following stations were added to Empire State's roster of TV stations: WNBC-4, WNYW-5, WABC-7, WWOR-9, WPIX-11, and WNET-13, following the unprecedented circumstances of September 11, 2001.

To accommodate the transmission, tenants in the 77th, 78th, and 79th floors cooperated in a relocation of their offices.[10] Wrote Minky Worden in a *Newsweek* web article:

*A few years ago, when I first joined the many thousands who work in the art-deco spire, my view took in all of lower Manhattan, stretched out in a shimmering arc. With the enthusiasm of the transplanted Tennessean that I am, I relished all opportunities to drag even unwilling visitors to the top—especially at sunset, when the pink and orange sky put the Twin Towers, the Statue of Liberty and Ellis Island into relief.*

*Since the attacks, my office is literally the pinnacle of the Manhattan skyline. As U.S. officials warn daily of new terrorist attacks on the horizon, there is anxiety about tall buildings in general, but about the Empire State Building in particular.*[11]

Since the events of September 11, 2001, New Yorkers swell with a feeling of pride and, indeed, a sense of ownership of the grandeur and ruggedness of the Empire State Building. Welcoming more than two million visitors a year, the Empire State Building, considered by many the most famous and revered skyscraper ever built, is now more than ever one of the city's best-loved icons.

*Empire State had lifted itself to "superb isolation, unbroken quiet, serene aloofness" as its twin brothers to the south succumbed on September 11, 2001.*

**Captivating for 70 Years**

New York was "The City" before the Empire State Building was built, but few can envision Manhattan without it. This cloud tickler has been called the city's exclamation point, the eagle feather in its cap, and 365,000 romantic tons of limestone, granite, steel, and marble. Despite its historic failure as a tremendous economic success, the Empire State Building's great fortitude and seemingly solitary presence reflect the feeling and spirit of New York City.

"Up there, among the clouds," said one history of the Empire State, "the drumbeat of New York is stilled, the nervous staccato of the city's life is left behind. In the superb heights of the Empire State, the mind is free. Here the real work which is the life blood of New York can be achieved restfully." [12]

For tourists, missing the Empire State Building is like going to Paris and skipping the Eiffel Tower or taking a trip to Egypt and bypassing the Pyramids.

Even without the amenities that visitors found in the 1930s—a lounge, writing room, soda fountain, cocktail bar, and tea room—the view from the observatory is still the best in the land, as New York spreads out like a tapestry beneath and the skyline forms a magic circle that encloses the tremendous, ceaseless vitality that is Manhattan. Perhaps it is the magic of having the world at their feet that continues to thrill people.

But not everyone comes for the view and very few for solitude among thousands of other visitors. Some just peek out at the world so they can say they've done it, others to imagine King Kong hanging on for his life. "I watched that movie [we're not sure which one, but probably *King Kong*], and ever since I was a kid I've wanted to come here and check this place out," Diego Armani, in town from Argentina, told Lola Ogunnaike of the *New York Daily News*. "I was supposed to be in New York last year to see the World Trade Center towers, but I missed them," Armani said, grimacing.

Mary Ellen Naughton, a Bronx native, celebrated a never-to-be-forgotten 18th birthday at the top of the Empire State Building, compliments of her boyfriend, who married her a few years later. "It was great," she says, recalling the romanticism of the celebration. Mary Ellen and her husband, Peter, hope to celebrate a significant upcoming wedding anniversary in the same way…taking in the aerial view of their native New York, where they spent so many memorable hours.

Ellie Rudd, a Queens native, went to the tallest building in the world during the New York World's Fair in 1939, when she was seven years old. The sensation of being on an open observation deck was quite different than, say, looking out from an airplane window. Rudd says, "I remember thinking I had better hold on to my glasses, afraid they would fall off, because I am blind as a bat without them!"

Empire State had lifted itself to "superb isolation, unbroken quiet, serene aloofness" as its "twin brothers" to the south succumbed, as chronicled in a poem by Edwin Torres.

## I Saw You Empire State Building

By Edwin Torres

I saw you Empire State Building
looking for your twin brothers
I saw you
watching your brothers burning
helpless to the ground
I look up at you, tall proud beacon
I too am a tower
it's my last name in Spanish

I look at you
glistening in the morning
shining at night I saw you
watching your brothers die
they were beautiful
and tall although
I think you have more character
but, older brothers wear their age well

I saw you helpless
and wanted to comfort you but
you're too big to hug
so I just keep looking at you
crying for you
holding you in my stare
us towers
we have to stick together [13]

## NOTES

### Introduction

1. Jonathan Goldman, *The Empire State Building* (New York: St. Martin's Press, 1980), p. 9.
2. Rudy Giuliani, Mayor of New York City, Press Release, February 12 , 1997, Archives of the Mayor's Press Office. www.nyc.gov/html/om/html/97/sp082-97.html.
3. W. A. Starrett in *Empire State: A Pictorial Record of Its Construction* (New York: William Edwin Rudge, 1931), p. 7.
4. E. Idell Zeisloft, *The New Metropolis*, 1899, reprinted in Museum of City of New York web pages, "Gotham Comes of Age." http://www.mcny.org/byron/GCAhome.htm. April 9, 2002.
5. Herbert Hoover quote reprinted in Stanley K. Schulz. Professor of History, in http://us.history.wisc.ued/hist102/lectures/ lecture18.html. April 15, 2002.
6. Ibid.

### Chapter 1

1. Empire State, Inc., *The Empire State* (New York: Publicity Association, 1931), p. 21.
2. Jonathan Goldman, *The Empire State Building* (New York: St. Martin's Press, 1980), p. 26.
3. Empire State, Inc., p. 21.
4. J. Carson Webster, "The Skyscraper: Logical and Historical Considerations," in *Journal of the Society of Architectural Historians* 43 (December 1959): pp. 126–139.
5. Professor Jeffrey Howe, Boston College. http://www.bc.edu/bc_org/avp/casd/fnart/fa267/skydef.html. April 22, 2002.
6. Janet Parks, Museum of the City of New York. http://www.mcny.org/hawley1.htm. April 15, 2002.
7. Goldman, *The Empire State Building*, p. 30.
8. Ibid.
9. Carol Willis, ed. *Building the Empire State*. W. W. Norton and Skyscraper Museum. New York: 1998, p. 20.
10. Empire State, Inc., p. 16.
11. Elizabeth Farrelly, *Sydney Morning Herald* 2001, http://stephenstenson.com/information/tower-power/tower-power.html.
12. Theodore James, Jr., *The Empire State Building* (New York: Harper and Row, 1975), p. 3.
13. "Notes on the Construction of the Empire State Building," in Carol Willis, ed.
14. Ibid.
15. Elizabeth Farrelly, *Sydney Morning Herald* 2001. http://stephenstenson.com/information/tower-power/tower-power.html. April 15, 2002.
16. G. E. Kidder Smith, *Looking at Architecture* (Harry N. Abrams, New York: 1990), p. 152.
17. William Starrett, essay in *Empire State, A Pictorial Record of Its Construction* (William Edwin Rudge, New York: 1931).
18. "Notes on the Construction of the Empire State Building," in Willis, ed.

### Chapter 2

1. Quote from Larry Schneider in Jeff Kisseloff, *You Must Remember This* (New York: Harcourt, Brace, Jovanovich, 1989), p. 72.
2. Will Rogers Company. http://www.cmgww.com/historic/rogers/quote.html. April 17, 2002.
3. Quote from Larry Schneider in Jeff Kisseloff, *You Must Remember This* (New York: Harcourt, Brace, Jovanovich, 1989), p. 131.
4. He believed it was called the Pilgrim Line. Sophia Tylutka thought it was a Cunard Line ship.
5. Interview with Theodore Baron, New York resident and employee, April 1990.
6. Frederick Simpich, "This Giant That Is New York," *The National Geographic Magazine*, Vol. LVIII, No. 5, November 1930.
7. Four hundred was the number of people said to fit in Mrs. Astor's ballroom. These were the elite of New York society.
8. Edward Robb Ellis, *The Epic of New York City* (New York: Cowar-McCann, 1966), pp. 413–415. A new Waldorf-Astoria opened on the block bounded by Park and Lexington avenues and Forty-ninth and Fiftieth streets on October 1, 1931.
9. Empire State, Inc., *The Empire State* (New York: Publicity Association, 1931), pp. 26–27.
10. Underground Media. http://u-media.org/Forgotten2.html. April 12, 2002.
11. Lewis Hine, *Men at Work* (Dover Publications: New York, 1977).
12. Freddie Langer in Lewis Hine, *The Empire State Building*, (Prestel: New York, 2001), p. 21.
13. Roland Maycock, "Purple," *The Magpie* (May 1929): p. 63, in http://newdeal.feri.org. Used with permission.
14. Leonard A. Hoffman, "Blood," *The Magpie* (May 1929): p. 63, in http://newdeal.feri.org. Used with permission.
15. Paul J. Elkin, "Shades," *The Magpie* (May 1929): p. 63, in http://newdeal.feri.org. Used with permission.

### Chapter 3

1. Frederick Simpich, "This Giant That Is New York," *The National Geographic Magazine*, Vol. LVIII, No. 5, November 1930.
2. Vernon Howe Bailey (with essay by William A. Starrett), *Empire State, A Pictorial Record of Its Construction* (William Edwin Rudge, New York: 1931), p. 29.
3. Starrett Corportion (corporate web site), http://www.starrettcorp.com/services. April 14, 2002.
4. Bailey (with essay by William A. Starrett), p. 2.
5. Empire State, Inc., *The Empire State* (New York: Publicity Association, 1931), p. 33.
6. *Engineering News Record*, 1999. http://www.enr.com/new/ A0419.asp.
7. Empire State, Inc., p. 4.
8. Ibid., p. 33.
9. Ibid.

### Chapter 4

1. Carol Willis, ed., *Building the Empire State* (New York: Skyscraper Museum and W.W. Norton, 1998), p. 11.
2. Term attributed to architect Vincent Scully.
3. Ann Banks, *First Person America* (New York: Alfred A. Knopf, 1980), p. 90.
4. Ann Banks, *Voices from the Thirties. Life Histories from the Federal Writers Project*. Transcript #22032106, http://rs6.loc.gov/wpaintro/thorsten.html. April 15, 2002.
5. All details about the construction of the Empire State Building are taken from the construction notes, reproduced in Willis, *Building the Empire State*.
6. Ibid., p. 40.
7. Ibid.
8. Ibid., p. 14.
9. Paul Starrett, *Changing the Skyline: An Autobiography* (New York: McGraw-Hill, 1938). Quoted in Willis, *Building the Empire State*, 2.

### Chapter 5

1. Frederick Simpich, "This Giant That Is New York," *The National Geographic Magazine*, Vol. LVII, No. 5, November 1930.
2. An Empire State Observatories brochure, 1939, gave the admission price as $1.10.
3. Lester A. Reingold, *Air & Space Smithsonian* (July 2000) reprinted in "ESB in the News." http://www.esbnyc.com/tourism/tourism_facts_esbnews_july2000.cfm?CFID=636719&CFTOKEN=45601221. April 13, 2002.
4. Quote attributed to John Tauranac, author of *The Empire State Building: The Making of a Landmark*.
5. Interview with Kathryn Buechele Schneider, April 22, 2002.
6. Interview with Theodore Baron, New York resident and employee, April 1990.
7. William Roberts, "Plane Hits Building—Woman Survives 75-Story Fall." http://www.elevator-world.com/magazine/archive01/9603-002.htm. April 22, 2002.
8. Real estate broker Elizabeth Martin quoted in article, "Vacant Space Triples in Empire State Building," (February 6, 2002), by John E. Zarnecki, *Architectural Record*. http://www.architecturalrecord.com/news/articles/empire.asp. April 13, 2002.
9. Samuel K. Moore, Special Report, "On the Air," http://www.specyrum.ieee.org/webonly/special/sept01/air.html. May 1, 2002.
10. Stephen A. Tole, General Manager, Empire State Building and Vice President, Helmsley-Spear, Inc. "Broadcasters Find Refuge Here." State of the Empire, Volume IX, Spring 2002.
11. Minky Worden, "The View from the Empire State Building," *Newsweek* article in http://www.msnbc.com/news/645458.asp.
12. Empire State, Inc., *The Empire State* (New York: Publicity Association, 1931), p. 7.
13. Edwin Torres, "I Saw You Empire State Building" (May 5, 2002): http://poetry.about.com/library/weekly/aa092501h.htm.

# BIBLIOGRAPHY

A&E Entertainment. *Empire State Building*, video, New York: 1994.

Bailey, Vernon Howe (with essay by William A. Starrett). *Empire State: A Pictorial Record of Its Construction*. William Edwin Rudge, New York: 1931.

Banks, Ann. *First Person America*. Alfred A. Knopf, New York: 1980.

Bonechi, Casa Edritice. *The Empire State Building and Manhattan Skyscrapers*. Florence, Italy.

Czarnecki, John. *Architectural Record*, February 6, 2002. http://www.architecturalrecord.com/NEWS/ ARTICLES/empire.asp.

Ellis, Edward Robb. *The Epic of New York City*, Coward-McCann, Inc., New York: 1966.

Empire State Corporation. *State of the Empire*. Summer 2001.

Empire State, Inc., *The Empire State*. Publicity Association, New York: 1931.

Empire State Observatories brochure, 1939.

*Engineering News Record*, 1999. http://www.enr.com/ new/A0419.asp.

Farrelly, Elizabeth. *Sydney Morning Herald*, 2001, in http://stephenstenson.com.

Giuliani, Rudy. Mayor of New York City Press Release, 2/12/97. http://www.nyc.gov/html/om/html/97/ sp082-97.html.

Goldman, Jonathan. *The Empire State Building*. St. Martin Press, New York: 1980.

Grun, Bernard. *Timetables of History*. Simon and Schuster, New York: 1982.

Hine, Lewis. *The Empire State Building*, with introduction by Freddie Langer. Prestel, New York: 1998.

James, Jr., Theodore. *The Empire State Building*. Harper and Row, New York: 1975.

Kaplan, Daile, ed. *Photo Story: Selected Letters and Photographs of Lewis W. Hine*. Smithsonian Institution Press, Washington D.C.: 1992.

Kearney, Paul. *New York Herald Tribune*. June 29, 1952.

Kisseloff, Jeff. *You Must Remember This: An Oral History of Manhattan from the 1890s to World War II*. Harcourt, Brace, Jovanovich, New York: 1989.

Kyvig, David. *Daily Life in the U.S., 1920–1929*. Greenwood Press, CT: 2002.

*The Literary Digest*, May 16, 1931.

Maycock, Roland, Leonard A. Hoffman, and Paul J. Elkin. *The Magpie*, May 1929. http://newdeal.feri.org.

Milholland, Terence V., Senior Vice President, Chief Technology Officer, EDS. Speech, "Managing the Extended Enterprise," delivered June 27, 2001, in Dallas, TX.

Mitchell, Joseph. *My Ears Are Bent*. Pantheon Books, New York: 2001.

Moore, Samuel K. Special Report, "On the Air." http://www.specyrum.ieee.org/WEBONLY/special/ sept01/air.html.

Moorhouse, Geoffrey. *Imperial City: New York*. Henry Holt and Company, New York: 1988.

Moscow, Henry. *The Book of New York Firsts*. Syracuse University Press, New York: 1995.

"Notes on Construction of Empire State Building," written c.1930, found in offices of HRH Construction (Starrett Brothers), p. 5. These pages are photocopied and included in Carol Willis, ed., *Building the Empire State*. Skyscraper Museum and W.W. Norton and Co., New York: 1998.

Ogunnaike, Lola. *New York Daily News*. March 3, 2002.

Pacelle, Mitchell. *Empire: A Tale of Obsession, Betrayal and the Battle for an American Icon*. John Wiley and Sons, New York: 2001.

Reingold, Lester A. *Air & Space Smithsonian*. July, 2000. http://www.esbnyc.com/tourism/tourism_facts_esbne ws_july2000.cfm?CFID=636719&CFTOKEN=45601 221.

Schulz, Stanley K. http://us.history.wisc.ued/hist102/ lectures/lecture18.html.

Simpich, Frederick. "This Giant That Is New York," *The National Geographic Magazine*, Vol. LVIII, No. 5, November 1930.

Starrett, Paul. *Changing the Skyline: An Autobiography*. McGraw Hill, New York: 1938.

Tauranac, John. *The Empire State Building: The Making of a Landmark*. Scribner, New York: 1995.

Torres, Edwin. http://poetry.about.com/library/weekly/ aa092501h.html.

Trachtenberg, Alan. *America and Lewis Hine*. Aperture, Inc., New York: 1977.

Transcript #22032106. http://rs6.loc.gov/wpaintro/ thorsten.html.

Velardi, Maria Elena, et al. *The Empire State Building*. Casa Editrice Bonechi, Florence, Italy.

Webster, J. Carson. "The Skyscraper: Logical and Historical Considerations," in the *Journal of the Society of Architecutral Historians*, vol. XVIII, December 1959. http://www.bec.edu.

Wertsman, Vladimir F. *New York: The City in More than 500 Memorable Quotations*. Scarecrow Press, Lanham, MD: 1999.

Willis, Carol, ed. *Building the Empire State*. W. W. Norton and Co. and The Skyscraper Museum, New York: 1998.

Winkleman, Michael. *The Fragility of Turf: The Neighborhoods of New York City*. State Education Department, New York State Museum, Albany, NY: 1986.

Wolner, Edward W. *International Dictionary of Architects and Architecture*. Randall J. Van Vynckt, editor, Vol. 2. http://www.geocities.com/SoHo/Studios.

Worden, Minky. "The View from the Empire State Building," *Newsweek*. http://www.msnbc.com/news/ 645458.asp.

Astoria (specialists in art deco furniture). http://www.astoriaartdeco.com.

The Museum of the City of New York (a guide to New York City). http://www.mcny.org.

20th Century History web site. http://history1900s. about.com.

Yale University web site. http://www.yale.edu/yup/ ENYC/triangle–shirtwaist.html.

Public Broadcasting Station web site. http://www. pbs.org.

Underground Media (discussions on news and politics). http://u-media.org/Forgotten2.html.

Starrett Corporation (leading real estate developer, whose founders built the Empire State Building). http://www.starrettcorp.com/services.

# INDEX

---